Lost Refugees Found In Christ

One Family's Story of Survival and Salvation Through the Grace of God.

By

Sara Daraie

Lost Refugees Found In Christ

One Family's Story of Survival and Salvation
Through the Grace of God.

By

Sara Daraie

Printed in The United States of America

Published By:

ISBN: 978-1-548307-29-5

DEDICATION

I want to Thank God for taking us through the trials and hardships we experienced, which brought us to salvation in Christ and a deep relationship with Him.

Today now that I have been living in United States for over 17 years I still look back on my Dutch family and long for our fellowship. I would like to say thank you to all the believers in Delft and Krimpen, and a special thank you to Pastor Blenk and the board members of the church in Delft for all their tireless work. I want to thank God for their presence in our lives because they always accepted us a member of their own spiritual families.

I also want to Give a special Thanks to Life Church who encouraged me to write this book, our prayer team that we had at Lee Benton's house which they also always encouraged me and supported me with their prayers, as well as MJ Daraie for his help in translation, L. Latini, as well as Farsid Seyed Mahdi and his parents.

TABLE OF CONTENTS

SPECIAL FOREWORD

This is an incredible true story of survival. From an upbringing in a Muslim family throughout the revolution in Iran, you will greatly be inspired as you follow their lives navigating from a fearful, highly restrictive and dangerous environment to faith and freedom.

With a little more than the clothes on their backs, and driven by their will to live, follow their captivating story of escape, hiding to avoid deportation and sudden death, experiencing medical tragedies, facing uncertainties, adjusting to life as refugees, often questioning their own decisions, and relying on one another in their quest for asylum.

As you read their harrowing story, you will be inspired by The Holy Spirit of God of our responsibilities towards those entangled in these cruel situations beyond their control.

Bishop Andrew Bills – Founder & CEO

The Holy Spirit Broadcasting Network (www.hsbn.tv)

SECTION 1

CHAPTERS 1-3

This incredible story of survival and ultimately salvation, begins by painting a picture of a young life lived in revolutionary Iran. We learn of Sara's upbringing in a Muslim family, and follow her through many hardships and discoveries.

By the age of 18, Sara meets and marries Amin. We then follow their dramatic first years as a married couple. Together they are learning to navigate their lives in an increasingly strict and dangerous environment.

They experience hardships from all angles; their families, the government, as well as medical tragedies. Through it all Amin and Sara begin to rely on each other and the love of their children for strength.

CHAPTER 1

I was born in Iran, and raised in a traditional Muslim family. I was 12 or 13 when the Shah fell during the Islamic Revolution, but the Muslim religion played a central role in our family long before that time. Interestingly enough, my father though a strong husband and good provider, was not the religious one in our home. He never prayed, and never participated in any of the Quran studies that most Muslim men are expected to do. His only connection to the Islamic faith was through his love for my mother. Through this love, and out of respect for her, he allowed his children to be raised in this way even if he didn't agree. My mother's passion for Islam and Allah would completely shape all of our lives, and would set me on a path to seek a connection with a high power at a very young age.

She had come from a traditionally religious family herself, and my mother was determined that her children would be devout in their faith as well. Some of my earliest memories are of weekly Quran studies that she hosted for women in our home. Because the Quran was written in Arabic and we could only understand Farsi, she would invite the professional holy women to teach us how to be good Muslims. One woman would come every week dressed in full hijab, with only her face exposed. Her two assistants, also wearing the hijab, would carry her purse, and wait on her every need. Unlike ministers in western countries, these holy women were paid by each family to share their message and knowledge with them, and paid very well at that. Everything we knew about the teachings and values laid out in the Quran came from these holy teachers.

We prayed in Arabic too, 17 times a day without fail. Two of these prayers were said together as a family while we did the cleaning ritual of Namaz. Once at noon exactly, and once in the afternoon we would complete the Namaz ritual. Each arm, hand, leg, and foot would be ceremoniously washed in the proper way to honor Allah. I was told that I should feel lucky that our prayer rituals were so relaxed, and that in Arabic countries people faithfully complete the Namaz 5 times a day without exception.

There were also even more demanding rituals like fasting that I couldn't escape even as a small child. I didn't understand why we were fasting, but I did it anyway. My mother used force when necessary, and I had been taught to fear the wrath of Allah himself. This was enough for any child to be on their best behavior.

Fasting was especially difficult for me however. My mother would wake me up in the middle of the night to make me eat. I would then be expected to fast until sunset of the next day. While I was at school I felt like I would collapse from hunger, so I secretly snuck food wherever I could. I was terrified of being caught, but the hunger would become stronger than my fear at times.

Of course, I always told my mother that I had kept my fast even when I hadn't. Luckily, she always believed me, but I couldn't stop thinking that Allah was watching me lie to my mother. Surely there would be a punishment for this behavior. I lived with a constant fear and anxiety about what his punishment might be. This was not a loving God, but rather a punisher that watched my every step, and recorded every mistake. This was the only God that I knew.

Despite all of this fear that had been drilled into my head, my heart still longed for a relationship with the Creator of the Heavens and Earth. I wanted so badly to connect with God, and to understand what others around me seemed to.

Surprisingly, even with all of the strict Islamic rules, I remember my younger childhood being very happy. I was the baby of the family, and my parents were crazy about me. I never doubted their love, and always felt very secure in our home. We still had birthday parties, and games, and treats just like any other family.

My happiness would not last forever though. Being the youngest, I also had many older siblings that looked after me and told me what to do. Ramin was the first born, and at 12 years older than me, he knew that he could easily control me if he wanted to. As our country was changing, so too was our family. Ramin was always religious, but as time went on he became a devout Muslim with even more radical ideals than our mother. Before too long, I found myself asking his permission for everything.

I remember on my 11th birthday, my mother had decorated our house for the celebration. Streamers and balloons were hanging throughout the house, and my mother even removed some of our family pictures to make room for more birthday decorations. There was one picture however, that I asked her not to take down. It was a poster of Yasser Arafat that hung on our living room wall. He was a hero to the Islamic movement at the time, and I knew that Ramin would object to taking it down for any reason. My mother said, "This is my house, and if I want to move the poster... I'll move the poster!"

She left for the grocery store shortly after decorating, and my brother came home while she was gone. He beat me for removing the poster. He punched me over and over in the lower back while wearing something like brass knuckles. He told me not to complain to our parents, and I didn't.

"If you say anything to mom and dad," he'd say, "I'll kill you!"

I started my period for the first time within a day or two after this and was terrified to tell my mother. I thought that it was because of the beating and that she'd surely find out. Eventually I told my mother and she explained it to me. I was so relieved that she didn't suspect my secret about the beating.

Later when I was around 14 years old Ramin joined a radical Muslim group, and my circumstances became even worse. He was more and more entrenched in Islamic teachings, and felt like it was his responsibility to make sure I followed the rules. He controlled my every move, and my parents never knew about the hell that I was living.

I could do nothing right, and the beatings became more frequent. Firstly, I was a woman and in their eyes, all women were all evil. The evil that comes with being a woman can't be removed, but my brother was determined to at least train me to be the best Muslim woman I could be. He would push my head up against the wall and yell at me for not reciting the Quran properly, and punish me for making any little mistake that went against their Islamic rules. I was living with a sense of terror always, and in addition to the religious monitoring he treated me like a slave whenever my parents weren't there to see.

It was the middle of the winter one year, when he told me to go outside and wash the dishes in the basin that was in our backyard. I thought that he must have been joking! It was freezing, and the ground was covered in a light layer of snow. We always did the dishes inside anyway. There was truly no good reason for me to go outside and freeze over the dishes. Ramin insisted though, and I had no choice but to obey. I sat at the ice-cold washing basin and scrubbed dishes until my hands and arms were practically frozen. They were a bright red color and tingling with sharp pains all the way up to my forearm. I could barely bend my fingers by the time I was through. All of this I continued to hide from my parents out of sheer fear of what my brother might do if I told anyone.

Once a neighbor had taken pity on me when Ramin had demanded that I make a traditional Persian dish called "Ashe Rashteh". It is a hearty soup that is popular during cold weather, and he had demanded that I make him a batch from scratch. This sort of demand was not out of the ordinary, but this time I was at a loss. I truly didn't know how to make this complicated dish. What could I do? I knew that if my brother came home and found the soup not to his liking, that I would be beaten for sure. It was then that our neighbor heard me crying in the back yard, and came over to offer her help. Thankfully she knew the recipe quite well, and made sure I prepared it properly. This was one of the first times that someone else noticed my hardship that I was enduring with my brother.

Other friends and neighbors would also eventually suspect something was wrong with me, and one even tried to bring it to my mother's attention. Eventually by the time I was 16 I was reaching my breaking point. It may be difficult for some to understand why it took me so long to tell my parents about my brother's abuse, but it's important to put my experience in the context of post Islamic Revolution terms. Ramin was a politically active young man that had become well respected in certain circles. His authority should not technically have been greater than my father's, but I was afraid of him and afraid of what might happen to me if I stood up against him.

The day did finally come however, when I didn't care about the consequences any longer. Whatever was going to happen to me was going to happen, but I had to finally tell my parents about my secret life of torture. I prayed that my parents would stand by me, and save me from my brother's abuse. One evening just before dinner I gathered my courage and did what I had thought was impossible, and told them what had been happening to me in their own house right under their noses.

It was a strange feeling to have this truth out in the open, and what happened next was a blur. My father was furious with Ramin. I was his littlest girl, and he was devastated after finding out about my secret. He blamed himself for not being able to see what had been happening, and it broke his heart that he had not been able to protect me. He and my mother kicked my brother out of the house, and I finally found a moment of mental peace.

Ramin then went to live with a few young men from the Islamic group, and became engaged rather quickly to one of their sisters. His wedding was an interesting mix of his radical friends, and our family, which seemed very relaxed in comparison.

It was a traditional Muslim ceremony held at the Islamic community center. There was no music, and absolutely no dancing allowed. This silence was so odd, and made our family very uncomfortable. Traditionally, Persian weddings are quite a celebration, and it just didn't feel right to be so solemn at what was supposed to be a joyous occasion.

Certain family members decided to celebrate anyway despite the restrictions. They clapped their hands, and began making music by tapping on the table, and stomping on the floor. This display of happiness and traditional Persian culture was immediately stopped by my brother and his friends. Our family was told to be quiet, and to obey the "no music" rule.

It was a strange time in Iran with so many different ideas about what was right, and what was wrong. My family was by no means progressive or westernized like many of the families living in Tehran before the Shah fell. The new Islamic rule was difficult to conform to even for a religious family like ours though, and as a young woman I found it difficult to do anything without being watched. My brother was gone, but the Islamic police were gaining more and more control. They could stop you for any reason, and as a single woman I couldn't do anything outside without an escort. It was for this reason that most of my life was lived inside my house where the Islamic police couldn't reprimand me.

I spent much of my time reading whatever books I could get my hands on, and volunteering at the hospital. By that time our country was at war with Iraq, and volunteering to help wounded soldiers was one of the few honorable activities a young woman could participate in. I did find enjoyment in these things, but as I approached my 18th birthday I was looking forward to moving out of my parents' home, and being able to start a new life as a married woman.

Therefore, I was so happy when I met a young woman in a dress shop that wanted me to meet her brother. She thought I might be just his type, and maybe he would want to marry me. Little did I know that this one chance meeting would change my life forever.

CHAPTER 2

Because I was unmarried I was required to be accompanied by a chaperone always outside of my house. It was for this reason that I often went shopping in town with my aunt or other family members. On a particularly nice day in late fall my aunt decided to take me to a ladies' shop to look for material, and other goods.

A nice woman who struck up a conversation with my aunt while we were browsing in her store owned the shop. She seemed to like me right away, and after we had only been there a short time, she told me that she thought I'd be a perfect wife for her brother Amin. This was how many marriages were arranged in Iran at the time. Two families would come together to agree that their son and daughter were a good match.

I didn't know Amin at all. I didn't even know what he looked like, but I was excited as we left the shop. After all that I had endured living at my parents' house, marriage was a welcome escape, and a chance to start a new chapter in my life as a wife and mother. We hurried home that day and told my parents what had happened.

Things moved quickly after that. Amin and his family came to our house the very next evening to have a proper meeting. He seemed to like me, and I thought he was very nice. We talked and got to know each other a bit, but all-in-all we would only see each other a total of three times before our wedding day. It was a little scary to put all my faith into a young man that I didn't know, but I too was young and very determined to be a good wife. Even with all the uncertainty, I felt that this was my chance to begin a new journey.

Of course, not all women's dreams came true after marriage. There was always a chance that the man you had chosen to trust could turn out to be a monster. Just a year before

I met Amin, my cousin married a man that turned out to be just that. I felt guilty because I had helped set them up, but it was not until the wedding night that he showed his true colors. The night of the wedding while the wedding party was sleeping at the groom's house, my cousin ran out of her room screaming at the top of her lungs. Of course, the entire house woke up only to see her covered in bit marks and ripped bedclothes. Her new husband was yelling, claiming that my cousin had not been a virgin. Of course, this wasn't true, but he kept yelling and saying that he had been tricked into marrying her. Her own sister turned on her and called their brothers to come over to the house with knives to kill her so their family name wouldn't be damaged.

My mother was the only one that stepped in to defend my poor cousin, and after a long conversation convinced the group to let her take her to the doctor to determine her virginity. Just as we assumed, the doctor confirmed that my cousin had been a virgin before her wedding, and that she had clearly been raped by her new husband. Her reputation was restored, but she was still going to have to try and live with this new husband and be a subservient wife. Divorce was never an option. Though this situation had scared me a bit about how some men can treat their wives, I had a good feeling about my new husband-to-be and never thought that I could be in a similar situation to my cousin. Besides, getting married and starting a family was our only option as women. It was what we were supposed to do, and I was excited to for my new life to begin.

At that time, most people held weddings inside their homes to avoid the Islamic rules against dancing, and singing. The Persian tradition of a lively wedding party was still very much important, but wasn't appropriate for a Mosque or Islamic center. If we kept our celebration private, the Islamic Police would not take interest in it.

Our wedding took place on December 7, 1983 when I was still just 18 years old, and Amin 24. It was very much a traditional

Persian celebration with both of our families celebrating together, and wishing us luck for the future.

We did not however go to a fancy hotel on our wedding night, or take off for a traditional honeymoon. Instead we stayed at Amin's parents' house where I had agreed to live while we saved money to get a place of our own. It wasn't uncommon in those days. Most Persian families expected their sons and their sons' wives to live with the family until they had enough money to purchase a house for themselves. Amin was the one that had suggested we rent a house instead of living with his family, but in the end his father won me over, and I agreed to live with them after the wedding.

It was a packed house, and even though I was eager to spend time with my new husband we ended up sitting and talking with his family a bit more after the wedding. In addition to Amin and myself, his parents already had 2 of their other sons living with them along with their wives and one baby boy. I didn't mind the close quarters though. It was exciting, and I was grateful to be out on my own.

My naïve happiness did not last long however. Later that same evening I noticed Amin began to look unhappy. Just by the way he was carrying himself I could tell something was wrong. Eventually he excused himself and went upstairs to our room. I must have looked confused because his mother told me that I should go after him and find out what was wrong.

I walked into our dark room to see Amin sitting in the corner crying. I was shocked. I immediately went to him and pleaded for him to tell me what was wrong. He looked up at me and simply said, "My brother. You are uncovered, and you were sitting there in front of my brother talking to him."

I had never heard of covering yourself with Hijab in front of a married family member, but I could tell that I deeply hurt him with my mistake. I also had no idea before this moment that my new husband was such a devout Muslim. In all our previous meetings, this fact had been hidden from me. I felt a little deceived as I realized that I had just married into a potentially worse situation than I had endured with my brother. There was no point in regretting it though. What was done was done. I was married to Amin, and it was my duty to obey his wishes as his wife.

He pulled out a full-length hijab with a headpiece much like Yasser Arafat wore, and told me that I must wear it always. The only time that I was permitted to take it off was to shower, and when I was in our room at night. I obediently told Amin that I would do as he wished, and apologized for my embarrassing mistake. I still had hope that he would be a good husband, but I had a feeling by then that my new life was going to be more difficult than I had previously thought.

Much like my brother, Amin had taken it upon himself to dive head first into the Islamic movement. His drive and commitment to his work proved a good fit for Islam as well, and he excelled in religious classes held at the Mosque for young men. Unfortunately for me this also meant that my worst fear had come true. I had married a man that was even more radical than my brother had been, and he would likely be influenced by many of the strict anti-female teachings that were popular within those circles. Instead of escaping my past and starting a new chapter in life I had just unknowingly given myself a life sentence, and there was no way out.

We lived with his family for the next 10 months. It was during this time that I learned just how important Islam was to Amin, and how his relationship with his family was second only in importance to his faith. Amin was a good boy all his life. The favored son from an early age, he started working at 10 years old and saved nearly every penny he earned. While his brothers were out spending their money on girls and nights out, Amin stayed home and saved his earnings for his future. His mother and sisters always fawned over him too. He would bend over backwards to help them in any way that he could, and they were used to being one of his top priorities. As his wife, I often felt like his family resented me for taking Amin's attention away from them. They wanted him to have a good wife, but I was to stay quiet and obey my husband. The radical Islamic movement may have made the situation for women worse in Iran, but troubles between a daughter-in-law and her husband's family was very much ingrained in Iranian culture too. Amin deserved only the best, and I could never hope to their vision of what a perfect wife could be.

I was trapped in our little bedroom most days just cleaning the same room over and over. My new husband once brought me a chamber pot and told me, "You eat here, and you go to the bathroom here! You do not leave this room!"

He would check the furniture each day by running his finger over the top to see if I had missed any dust, and I couldn't take the chance that he might not approve of the cleaning job I had done. Plus, I wasn't permitted to talk to anyone in his family without him being there so there wasn't much else I could do. I was not even allowed to speak to my sister-in-laws freely. He was afraid that their attitudes toward their husbands might "rub off on me". He thought that they were lazy, and didn't want his wife to become that way too. He had married me to be the good, obedient woman whom he could mold into the perfect Muslim wife.

My only option was to try and please him, and he made sure I knew when he was displeased. Shortly after we were married he had come home early to find our room not up to his standards, and he beat me horribly in response.

In that instant, all my hopes for my future were shattered. My dream of freedom through marriage had turned into a nightmare, and I knew that violence would once again be something I'd have to endure. Everyday became a waiting game to see if I had done something that deserved a beating. I didn't understand how a man that could have so much love toward his mothers and sisters could ever treat his wife this way. Over the next few months I would be thrown against walls, kicked, and bruised countless times. It was an unspeakably horrible time in my life. A time ruled by fear, with little else to cling to.

We eventually did move into our own rented house just down the street from Amin's family. It was a nice lower level apartment that was part of a larger estate. I was still dealing with physical abuse once we moved, but at least I had my own space and wasn't confined to our bedroom like before. It was shortly after we moved that I also gave birth to our first child. I had gotten pregnant shortly after we were married, and before our first wedding anniversary our son had arrived.

Our baby MJ was my miracle, and my purpose for living. I knew that even if I had to endure the torture of physical abuse and control, my son would give me a reason to keep on living. I also knew that Amin was, to his core a family man, and that he would put our children above all else. The love that I saw Amin give to MJ gave me hope for my situation too. He was always eager to help with the baby even in the middle of the night. I could see that he truly loved being a father and these moments made me believe that there was something behind all his anger and violence toward me. I felt like the real man was in there somewhere just waiting to get out. It is hard to believe, but he had a gentleness of spirit that came out with MJ, and I prayed that someday it would break down the walls that he had built up around himself.

For the next year, though, life went on as it had before. The beatings were still frequent, but I was getting better at not making mistakes, and tried to focus on the good parts of my life. What I didn't know was that the worst was still to come.

CHAPTER 3

God blessed me with a second pregnancy when MJ was just 2 months old, but I would never get to meet my second son. It began when Amin and I got in to an argument over something his father had said to me. I was about six months along at the time. My sister-in-law was going to take me with her to the public bath later that day, and I asked my husband when he would be home to watch MJ. My father-in-law didn't approve of how much Amin was doing to help with the baby, and decided to poke fun at his son because of it.

He said to me," I feel like you're going to have to buy my son a bra so he can nurse the baby too!"

His insult made it uncomfortable for everyone in the room, and I left shortly after. Amin stayed behind, and would meet me at our house later. I'll never know what was said after I left, but Amin came home very angry. He blamed me for speaking to his father improperly, and accused me of having no respect for him as my husband. He beat me very badly that night, much worse than even I had become accustomed.

I clearly remember lying on the ground being kicked repeatedly in the back. I was praying for the safety of my baby, and tried my best to protect my belly. He broke my nose that night too. The blood poured out of my face onto our mattress, and wouldn't stop. Amin had to throw the mattress away because of the amount of blood that had soaked into it. It was at that point the next morning that he decided to take me to the hospital.

The doctor could see that something wasn't right, and was concerned for my safety right away. I assured him that I had simply fallen and hit my face, but he pressed Amin for answers too. Spousal abuse was accepted in Iran at that time to a certain extent in private, but it was still important to keep up appearances while out in public.

"Is she your wife?" The doctor asked, "Who did this to her?"

Amin lied right in front of me and told the doctor that he was my brother, not my husband. He said that he had no idea what had happened, and it was left at that.

They treated my broken nose and examined my bruised eyes. Then gave me an ultrasound to check on the baby, and because of a sharp pain I had in my back. I knew something was not right. They told me that I had a small tear in the wall of my placenta, and that the amniotic fluid was leaking. The doctor put me on bed rest for the next three months of my pregnancy and sent me home. I did exactly what the doctor told me to do, and went to live with my mother while anxiously awaited my due date.

A little over four weeks later I went into early labor. The baby was seven and half months by then, and the doctor thought there was a good chance that the baby would be born without any issues. However, all the careful waiting and bedrest was not enough in the end to save my second son. When he was born, he wasn't breathing properly and they put him on my chest to get him close to my heartbeat and to feel the warmth of his mother's body. They then worked on him for nearly two hours right there in my room. I saw everything. They wanted to take him away, but I wouldn't let them. I fought to stay with my baby until the doctors finally gave up. The rest of the time in the hospital was a blur full of depression and disbelief.

My spirit was devastated after that. It took weeks to recover physically, but my heart would always be broken. I had never spoken to anyone openly about my abuse from my husband, but by then my family could suspect what was going on. Amin's sister who lived on the outskirts of town with her family also tried to help me, but there was little anyone could do. They offered to bring me to their homes to help watch over MJ while I recovered, but in the long-term I would have to return to my life with Amin. Divorced women were the lowest class of women in Iran, and had absolutely no rights. If I left him I would have to move back in with my parents, and live the rest of my life alone. I would have no rights to our kids, and no rights to our money. No, it was better to deal with it as best as I could for the sake of MJ.

After a month past life was starting to get back to normal. I was finally able to stand on my feet for most of the day like before, and was back to cooking and cleaning in our home. MJ was 11 months old getting ready to celebrate his first birthday, and I was beginning to find joy in being a mother again. My neighbor helped me with more complicated errands like grocery shopping because I was still not well enough to be out in public alone. She had a young daughter around the age of 10 that would tag along with us, and help with the little things. They were a big help to me, and I was so grateful to have them.

On this particular day, we had just returned from the grocery store when my neighbor's daughter was laying MJ down on his pillow that was on the floor. She must have taken a misstep and as she was lowering him down, he missed the pillow and cracked his head on the stone floor. It was nothing out of the ordinary, and the distance that he fell could have been measured in inches. I made sure he was ok, and didn't give it much thought.

We went on putting the groceries away, but noticed that MJ wouldn't stop crying. He had gotten a vaccination a few days before, and I thought he might have been overly sensitive because of the shot, but as time went on I knew he wasn't acting like himself. The crying was getting worse, and he began to projectile vomit all the food I gave him. By the time Amin got home the house had not been cleaned and I hadn't any time to prepare any meals. He told me to forget about the house, and to take care of the baby. "Maybe he needs to sleep," Amin suggested.

We both tried to calm him down, but soon we knew he had to be seen by a doctor and left for the urgent care close to our home. There the doctors told us that MJ was slipping into a coma. We were shocked.

The next 24 hours were a roller coaster of emotions, and seemed like a surreal nightmare. We had left the urgent care for the hospital, and by the end of the day the doctors concluded that MJ's brain had been badly bruised by the fall causing blood to fill his skull. They told me to take him home and wait for him to die, and that he may not even make it to the first stop light on the way home. What is there to do when the doctors have just told you that your son, your only reason for living, is going to die? I was in a state of shock, but I persisted, and was determined not to give up on my son. I couldn't live with myself if I didn't at least try to fight for his life, even if it was unlikely that he would live.

By coincidence, Amin's brother knew a surgeon from another hospital, and arranged for him to come and look at MJ. His diagnosis was just as grim, but he was willing to at least try and relieve some of the pressure on his skull by performing brain surgery. He brought together a team of 5 surgeons from around the city to perform the complicated procedure. One of the surgeons was a woman and had her young son with her when she got to the hospital. We had to look after him during the long five-hour surgery. It was welcome escape from the torture of waiting, and anticipation I would have been focused on otherwise.

The doctors finally came out nearly five and a half hours later, and stood silently in front of me and the rest of our family that had come to the hospital by then. Amin was there, along with my mother as well. We waited for the news. They explained that the surgery had technically been a success because he was still alive, and was not entirely brain dead, but it was going to be a long night. MJ would need constant supervision over the next 10 hours, and nothing was for sure. He might still die, or lose his brain function completely before the night was over. I insisted that I be the one at his bedside that night. My mother and Amin's sister insisted that I come home with them to rest, but that was not an option for me. He was my only child, and my only source of joy. He was my life, and I was going to be there to help him, or be there to comfort him if he didn't make it through the night. The doctor could see my determination and agreed that I would be the best person to keep vigil at the hospital.

Through the long night I kept constant watch over my baby. I cried, and prayed harder than I ever had before in my life. I made sure he was comfortable, but more than anything I begged God for a miracle. We weren't supposed to pray directly to God. I had always been taught that I wasn't worthy and that the prophets were our middlemen that talked to God for us. That night I tried everything though. I was desperate. I didn't even care about the abuse any more. I didn't care about how difficult my life was. All I wanted was to see my son get better, and I was truly willing to sacrifice everything for him, even my life.

The minutes seemed to stretch on and on, but eventually morning came, and by a true miracle of God MJ was still alive. The doctors were shocked that he had survived.

"He is through the worst of it," they said, "It will be a long time before we know what damage his brain may have sustained, but he's alive, and seems to have normal brain functionality."

I burst into tears of joy and disbelief. "Thank you God!" If there was ever a time for my prayers to be answered, this would have been the only prayer I hoped God heard. MJ was alive, and he was out of immediate danger. That was all that I cared about.

Shortly after we got the good news from the doctor, my mother was insistent that I leave the hospital to clean up and rest. I had been there for nearly 2 days without any rest so I agreed that it was time for a break. Amin's sister begged me to come to her house and rest there. She had this look in her eyes like she was trying to protect me. She knew what I had been suffering with because of Amin's abuse, and I could see that she was afraid that he might blame me for MJ's accident. I knew that she might be right. I had no reason to believe that Amin would have any other reaction. It was the life that I was used to living.

"No Sara," Amin's sister said, "You have to let me take care of you. If you go home, he might kill you."

Amin would not listen to any of it though. He insisted that I was his wife, and that I was to come home with him only. So, I did. I gave MJ a kiss on his forehead left the hospital to meet my husband at home. I didn't know what would be waiting for me when I got there, but I no longer cared really. I was so thankful that MJ was alive that I had little room in my head for fear.

SECTION 2

CHAPTERS 4 - 6

After one tragedy after another, Sara and Amin keep moving on, building strength through their love and commitment to each other. The political environment in Iran is getting worse though, and the young family begins to fear what might become of their young sons if they stay in Iran.

By Chapter 5, Sara and Amin have decided to risk everything and escape to The Netherlands to claim asylum. This is no easy feat, and the couple jumps through hoops to try and figure out the best way to safely leave for The Netherlands.

After making it successfully to The Netherlands, the young family finds themselves alone in multiple refugee camps wondering if they had made the right decision.

CHAPTER 4

I awaited Amin's arrival in our empty home. It was quiet, and I could imagine MJ playing in the living room. Sitting there alone the emotions of the last few days finally caught up with me. I cried awhile just as a release of everything I had been through. I thanked God over and over again. I wasn't sure why he was showing me his mercy, but I considered it a true miracle that my baby had survived.

I took a shower and freshened up, then heard a knock at my door. Amin's sister, the one that always tried to protect me, was standing on my doorstep looking anxious. I didn't want to imagine why she could be there, so I opened the door to face whatever it could be. She rushed through the entrance and grabbed my hand.

"What?" I said impatiently, "What is it?"

She kept hold of my hand and looked at me as a smile spread across her face.

"Amin has gotten into an argument with our parents," she almost whispered. "He's on his way over right now."

"What? Why?" I asked, "What do you mean a fight?"

"He has gotten into an argument with our father and told him that if he can't treat you with respect then he won't be bringing MJ over to see him when he recovers!"

At first I wasn't quite sure what to make of what she had said. Why would Amin go over to fight with his father over this? Why now? I was confused, yet also curious as to what might happen when Amin got home.

She then explained how he had spent the entire night, sitting alone in their basement crying. None of them had ever seen him act that way before. I realized that while I had been crying at our child's bedside, begging God for a miracle, my husband had been going through his own emotional conversation with God. Maybe we had shared prayers that night. Maybe this horrible event had given him a glimpse into what really mattered. I didn't know what to think exactly, but I felt myself feeling hopeful about what his reaction would be.

My sister-in-law left quickly through the front door and I hurried to look out the back to see if he was coming down the alley. Sure enough he was rounding the corner, and I ducked back inside.

I hurried over to the kitchen to prepare the tea that I had already made, when the door swung open. He came into the house silently and sat down on the couch. I took the tray with two cups on it over to where he was in our living room. As I bent over to serve him, he put his hand on my hand very gently.

"I know that last night was very hard for you Sara," he said. He looked directly into my eyes and continued, "I don't want you to worry about taking care of the house or anything else. I just want you to take care of yourself."

I nodded my head in agreement as tears welled up in my eyes. I couldn't believe that he wasn't angry.

He didn't cry or beg for forgiveness, he just treated me kindly with great compassion and understanding. After that day my husband was truly a new man. Something had happened that night when MJ was in the hospital. It was as if nearly losing his son had made him see the situation more clearly. Not only did he stand up for me among his family after that, he also began to treat me like I mattered. We began building a partnership, and he never hit me again after that.

I wasn't the only one who couldn't believe Amin's change of heart. Our neighbors came to the hospital to look in on MJ and were almost happier to see me alive, than him. They all knew what had been going on, and were relieved to see that their fears did not come true.

"We were praying for you!" They'd say, "Thank God you are O.K."

As time went on MJ continued to recover. He progressed mentally and physically, with little signs of the accident at all. We had to monitor him closely for the first six months. He wasn't allowed to run or walk without supervision, and we were supposed to keep his movement completely controlled. For a toddler, this type of restriction was torture, and almost impossible to stick with, but together with help from our families, we watched as our son came back to us. He would be on medication for five years after that, and always be at risk for seizures, but that was a small price to pay compared to what we could have lost.

Amin had purchased a piece of land outside of the city, and began preparing to build us a house there. For the first time in my life, I was happy. Amin was turning into the husband that I knew he could be, the husband that I wanted so badly. I was so thankful for every moment.

By that time the Iran and Iraq War had started to heat up, and the city of Tehran wasn't as safe as it once was. This drove Amin to work intently on the new house in order to finish it as soon as possible. He worked on it constantly, and did almost every portion by himself. MJ and I would come to the site too. We would do little odd jobs to help move things along, and together as a family we built our dream house.

After a long building process, we moved into our new home when MJ was three years old. It was a beautiful house with three bedrooms upstairs that overlooked the garden and mountains in the distance. We built the basement as a stand-alone apartment with a separate kitchen and dining area. This made it easy for us to go on living our lives if there were threats of bomb strikes because of the war. We were also able to offer shelter to our families there when Tehran became too dangerous.

In fact there were a few times when we had five or six of our siblings and their families staying with us during the war. It may have seemed like an imposition to anyone else. But we loved having them there. I always cooked for the whole group, and Amin made sure they were all comfortable. The war was a stressful time for everyone, and we wanted to make things as easy as possible. They would just bring their suitcases and show up like they were going on vacation, and they all knew there were welcomed any time.

In spite of the war, it was a great time in our household. If relatives weren't staying downstairs they were always coming over for a party or family dinner, and MJ was back to being a normal little boy. Amin was working hard and doing very well financially, and our relationship was blossoming into a truly great partnership. Things may have been good inside our house, but the outside world seemed to be getting worse.

After just three months in our new house, Amin volunteered to join the Iranian army. He spent 40 days near the front lines taking wounded men back and forth from the hospital. The government was really pushing for all men to "do their duty", and help in the war effort. Of course Amin, being the obedient type of man that he was, felt strongly about offering help to the men that had seen the worst part of the fighting. He came back with a slightly different view of the situation however, and that was one of the turning points in which he started loose faith in the system of our country. I had learned by then that Amin had a very generous heart, and that generosity spread to his work with the soldiers as well. He was disappointed to see that they were not treated quite as kindly by the same government they had sacrificed for though. He came back even more determined to focus on me and our family, to make our home a true sanctuary where the problems of the outside world could be forgotten.

Amin had been back from the war for almost nine months, and we had been living in our house away from Tehran just over a year when we suffered another devastating setback that threatened to take away the nice life we had built for ourselves.

It was mid-afternoon just before the end of the workday when I went out to grab a few things from the store for a party we were having later that night. I was driving home on my way back from the shop when my car was blindsided by a huge truck. The truck hit my side of the car and completely ran me off the road. I don't remember exactly what happened after that, but I knew that it was bad. I knew that I had been hurt pretty severely, and honestly wasn't sure I would survive as I sat watching the police working on the car. By coincidence, Amin was coming home at that very same time. He was looking over of the line of cars that had become backed up, and saw that it was an accident. Somehow he was able to notice that it was me that had been crushed, and he ran to the scene. He dealt with the police, and the truck driver that had caused the accident, but was mostly concerned for my safety and went with me in the ambulance to the hospital.

I woke up in a hospital bed covered in tubes, and in more pain then I ever thought was possible. I had broken nearly every bone in my lower body including my hip and pelvis, and could barely move. Because all of my bones were broken, there was no support left to hold in many of my internal organs, and they had fallen through my pelvic floor and were outside of my body.

The doctors were not optimistic about my recovery. They weren't even sure if I would ever be able to walk again. The war had complicated matters even further as a majority of the best orthopedic surgeons were on the battlefield attending to the wounded soldiers. The doctors at the hospital did their best, but my hip was not set properly, and I was intense pain for years after the accident because of it. It also made my recovery even more difficult.

I was in the hospital for two straight months, and then moved into my parents' house so my mother could help take care of MJ. Amin was so broken hearted while I was in the hospital that he sold our beloved dream home. He said that he couldn't bear to be there anymore, that it reminded him too much of me and the good times we had had there.

He was an absolutely devoted husband during that time. I was so thankful that he was determined to help bring me through my recovery, and was surprised at just how committed he was. It was when we decided to move in with Amin's parents' for a while that I realized just how much Amin had been dealing with to support me.

We had moved our belongings into their home, and Amin had left for work. I could tell they were not happy to have us there, and were certainly not going to help take care of me in any way. I still couldn't walk and barely felt my legs most times. I had to use my upper body to drag myself across the floor if I wanted to move anywhere throughout the house. We had only been there a few hours when my mother-in-law gathered up my bags and had Amin's father bring me outside with MJ. She said that she couldn't take care of me, and that I had to leave. I was panicked of course. What was I going to do? I couldn't even move properly, and they were pushing me out the door into a taxi with my small child.

I pleaded with them, crying, "Please no! Don't send me away until Amin gets home!"

They didn't want to hear it though, and said that we were too much of a burden for them to handle. They stuffed us into the taxi, and closed the door on my tear-stained face. We drove away not knowing where we'd go.

There were no cell phones at that time, and my family lived on the other side of the city. I knew that if Amin came home to find me gone he would first look at his sister's house. The sister who had tried to protect me when Amin was so cruel would be the first place he'd look. So that's where we went. To my surprise she was waiting with her husband outside the house when we pulled up. She looked sad, and angry. She opened the door and told me that she was sorry, but that we wouldn't be able to stay with them either. Amin's parents had called her and convinced her that she must stand with them. I begged and pleaded to let me stay until Amin came. At first she wouldn't agree, but eventually decided that she would let us in to wait for my husband.

It may seem strange to outsiders to hear about this type of treatment. It was not normal within the traditional Persian culture either. However, under the tenants of Islam, a wife who can no longer perform her duties is not a wife worth keeping. Amin had the right to divorce me if he wanted to because my handicap had made it impossible for me to be a good wife. Actually he had the right to take up to four wives as long as he could provide for them. As far as Amin's family was concerned, I was useless, and by not giving us help, they hoped that Amin would feel so overwhelmed that he would just give up. Then he would get rid of me to marry a younger, more capable woman.

Amin did come to his sister's that night, and never wavered in his commitment to our family and me. We left the next morning to stay at my parents' home again. My mother took care of me on every level. Just getting through the everyday tasks of life was nearly impossible, and without her help I would have been totally alone. We had to transfer to two of my brother's homes during construction at my parents', and experienced much of the same harsh treatment that Amin's family had given us. Their wives treated me like an outcast, and insisted that they would not be the ones helping to take care of me.

This was a very hard time emotionally for all of us. After all of the help, and generosity that we had shown our families before my accident, the fact that they would treat us this way was absolutely heart breaking. It was as if they were ashamed of me for being handicapped. Through it all Amin stood by me and pushed me to focus on my healing.

We'd eventually end up at my sister's house after I began walking with the assistance of a walker, then eventually moved to our own small apartment on the west side of Tehran. My body had come a long way in recovery. My organs were all where they were supposed to be, and I no longer had to crawl on the floor, but the pain was constant and intense.

CHAPTER 5

I was lucky to be alive. I was also lucky that my husband had stuck by me through my recovery. The residual pain was still constant years later, and served as a reminder of the accident but I focused on the positive things in my life. Things were going well and eventually we moved to a very nice area of Tehran on the North side. Amin had steadily built his handyman business, and it appears we might finally be able to enjoy our lives and our family together without something horrible happening.

The doctors were impressed with my progress, but thought that my pain may never fully go away. My main physician surprised me during one visit, and asked if I wanted more children. I was taken off guard and answered, "Of course I would love to have more, but I didn't think it would be possible after the accident."

While I had been told previously that another baby might kill me, or not be possible at all, he seemed to think that the pressure from the pregnancy might have been exactly what my body needed to put my hip back into Alignment. "I think if might be good for you to have another baby. The pressure might act as a natural form of traction, and decrease your pain."

I was overcome with joy at the possibility of having another child. I rushed home that day excited to tell Amin the good news. He was hesitant at first, and worried that the doctor may not be correct in his assessment. After all that we had been through, I know that he was worried that it might make my pain worse instead of better. I told him that we should put our trust in the doctor and in God, and that another baby would be an answer to my prayers in so many ways. Eventually he agreed, and I was pregnant with our son Omid two months later.

This pregnancy was much different than my pregnancy

with MJ, and light years away from the problems I had with my second pregnancy. Of course, the environment I was living in was much different than the last time, and our family dynamic was much more relaxed and loving, but this pregnancy was also different physically. I had been very sick when I was pregnant with MJ, but this time around I felt amazing. Amin hired someone to help me around the house, and even hired a driver to take MJ to school. All so I could enjoy my pregnancy, and take care of my body during the process. It was hard to believe sometimes, but my dream of having a loving husband and family was finally falling into place. After all the hardships that I had endured over the previous 10 years of my life I had nothing to complain about. I had my health, and my family. What more could I ask for?

Again, life inside our home was idyllic, and our extended families even came back around after a while. Amin's brothers, 2 of the same family members that shunned us after my accident, began coming to our house every workday for lunch and would spend time there even when I wasn't home. Our house was always full of life and food. It was a fun and happy place, and the regular family gatherings soon became a normal occurrence again. Life on the outside, however, had been progressively getting worse since the Islamic Revolution, and was beginning to cause problems for average people like us.

By the time that we lived in our little apartment on the Northern side of Tehran, the Iran Iraq War was over, and without a common enemy to pin the country's troubles on the government was beginning to see unrest among a dissatisfied public. To keep a tight hold on the people's behavior, the Islamic Police was used to intimidate and scare normal everyday citizens into submission. Everything you did outside of your house was scrutinized, and monitored. And when they couldn't find any legitimate reason for the harassment, they simply made up a reason.

Northern Tehran was also where the Ayatollah Khomeini

lived. In fact, his palatial estate was just two or three blocks from our home. At first we felt an added layer of security being so close to the Ayatollah, but soon discovered that it was more of a nuisance than anything else. Security was tight in our neighborhood, and the entire area was shut down once a year on our leader's birthday. It was always an enormous celebration that shut down most of the city, but especially the streets around our house. It was just another example of the power that the government had over us. Of course, we all were expected to go along with the celebration, or be under suspicion by the Islamic Police.

The little annoyances like this were not the biggest problem though. We started to notice the level of harassment was increasing, and the overall attitude of the people around us was changing. Our country was becoming radical, and those that weren't radical weren't allowed to speak up anymore. This state of constant fear that we were all living under caused people to behave strangely, and almost turn against each other for fear of doing something that would upset the Islamic monitors.

One afternoon after Omid was born, I came face to face with this harassment. We were out running errands in town when an Islamic Police officer stopped me. I was wearing my full hijab that all women were required to wear in public, and couldn't possibly think of a reason why he might have stopped me. He grabbed my arm and pointed at my baby. I looked up at him confused.

"What is that hat doing on your baby?" He yelled at me.

It was then that I realized that what I had thought was a cute little baby hat, had been perceived as a very "western-style" hat by this man. I immediately apologized for my offense, but he was not satisfied. He continued to berate me in public, and finally after a long scolding told me that he would put me in jail if he saw us out in this sort of offensive clothing again. I knew that he was not kidding. It may sound unbelievable, but we knew by then that this type of encounter was not a joke. The Islamic Police had every right in the world to accuse you of anything, and our rights were nearly non-existent. This was just the beginning, and we would have to endure much more before it would finally become too much for our family to handle.

My husband Amin was not immune to this harassment either. He was such a devout Muslim, and had given so much of himself to his country that I often couldn't believe the type of horrible treatment he received in our later years in Iran. His change in attitude toward our government, and ultimately our religion, first began after he returned from the war. He was shocked at the brutality of the situation, and was greatly affected by the hardships that many of our soldiers had to endure after they returned.

He was always involved with our community, and tried to help people whenever he could. Veterans were one group that he was very passionate about helping. There was one man that had lost his leg during the war, and couldn't get the government to give him a prosthetic. He had been waiting for nearly a year when Amin decided to help him. They went down to the administrative office together to see if Amin could speed up the process. He was shocked by the reaction of the government worker. Instead of praising the man for his service, he yelled at Amin and the veteran, and accused them of trying to get something for free that he didn't deserve.

"Oh you lost your leg so now you want the government to give you a new one for free?"

This was the kind of deranged logic that we had to deal with daily. None of us were safe from this type of bizarre thinking. Anyone could accuse you of anything, and twist any situation to suit their own motives. It was truly scary, and we lived our lives constantly walking on eggshells, making sure we didn't catch the attention of anyone. This went on for years, and progressively got worse.

One night, a few years after we had moved into our nice house on the North Side of Tehran, something happened that made us realize just how serious the climate was getting in our country.

Amin was eating his lunch in a public park when two Islamic Police officers approached him. Without much explanation, they arrested him and took him to the jail. He was told that he was under suspicion for drug possession and had no idea how long he would be held. I was a wreck. I had no idea where my husband was the entire day. All I knew was that he left for work that morning and never came back. I feared the worst had happened. I thought that maybe we had done something that made the wrong person angry, and that I'd never know what happened to him. Luckily they ended up letting him go later that same day in the middle of the night, but we knew then that we were on their radar.

I couldn't believe that a man like Amin could have enemies like this. A man that had taught Quran classes, and served his country in war was now treated like a common criminal without any evidence at all. It was horrifying to both of us, and this was when we began to think about leaving Iran. It was clearly no longer safe, and not only did I fear for my safety, but I knew things would only get worse as our boys got older. I didn't want to raise my children in an environment of fear like that. And what if they made a mistake? Would they end up in jail too, or maybe worse? No, it was time to do something for the sake of our children.

There weren't many options for Iranians to immigrate at that time. Our country would not allow us to travel abroad if they thought it was for any other purpose other than tourism. People were finding ways though. Amin's brother had legally moved to the Netherlands the year we had gotten married, and we knew of others that had recently gotten visas to travel there, and then claimed asylum to stay. It was something I had never considered growing up. I never thought that I'd leave Iran, but the culture had changed, and we decided to at least try to get out while it was still possible.

Amin contacted a man that secured travel visas to Europe to see if he could help us. We paid him well, and in exchange he could get visas for Amin, Omid, and myself but they wouldn't give them to MJ at the same time. This is when reality started to sink in. If we wanted to do this, if we wanted to leave, it wasn't going to be easy.

Amin and I were both scared. If we left Iran at different times there was no guarantee that we'd ever be reunited. What would I do if MJ and I were left behind permanently? There was a lot on the line, and a lot that could go wrong, but in the end, we decided that the risk was worth it. Amin discussed our options with the man that dealt with the visas, and paid him a significant amount of money to setup things with his connections at the airport. They also met with the Dutch Embassy that assured Amin that we would be able to claim asylum. They planned to try to get me on the plane with my visa and have MJ go on board without one. We would leave three weeks after Amin and Omid. If we could make it work, our family could live our lives safely and securely, and it would all be worth it.

So, we watched as Amin and Omid left for the airport, knowing that it would be almost three weeks until we saw each other again. Maybe longer if the plan didn't go as we hoped. They waved goodbye, and I imagined what it would be like when I saw them again. Where would we be? How long would it be? The anticipation ate me up the entire time that I was in Iran alone.

The first part of our plan fell right into place. Amin and Omid had made it safely to the Netherlands, and claimed political asylum once they were there. The authorities had granted it to them, and they were placed in a large refugee camp in Den Haag, southwest of Amsterdam. Amin had told me that it was an overcrowded mess, but at least they were there and hadn't been sent back to Iran. The first step of the plan had worked, now it was time for MJ and I to make our journey to join them.

I left for the airport with MJ in tow; fully knowing that while I had my visa my son did not have his. This could be the one glaring sign that could get us caught. The man that handled these things for us had told me to act confidently, and that no one would suspect that anything was amiss.

"If you believe it, they'll believe it," he said to me. "Just be respectful and don't show any fear. They can sense fear a mile away."

I wasn't sure what would happen to me if the authorities caught us. I couldn't think about that. I just focused on the plan, and tried to make myself believe that we had nothing to hide.

We entered the airport in Tehran. They didn't ask for the visa right away. I figured because the man we had paid had many connections at the airport that we'd be ok going through the first section of security. You could pay for anything in Iran, fake birth certificate, and fake passport. If you had the money anything was possible. After a few moments, we made it through initial security without much of a problem, and went into the boarding area of the airport.

I was still using my cane at the time, and had it with me as we sat waiting to board the plane. As we sat waiting for our plane to board, two women dressed in full black hijab approached us looking very stern.

They abruptly shouted, "Stand up! Follow us!"

I did as I was told, though I wasn't sure why they had singled me out of the crowd. They led us away from the boarding area and began to interrogate me.

"What's in your cane?" They snapped.

I looked up at them and calmly answered, "My cane?

Nothing, it's just a cane."

They snatched the cane away from me and proceeded to try and take it apart. My heart was pounding a million miles a minute. I knew there was nothing in that cane, but I was terrified they come up with something to delay our trip, or maybe they'd start asking questions and figure out that we only had one visa between us. I kept calm on the outside though. I was determined not to show them my fear.

I told them that if they had another cane that they'd prefer me to use, that was ok. I showed them notes from my doctor and x-rays showing the extensive damage I had sustained during the accident. I told them that my reason for my trip was to seek advanced medical help from doctors in Holland. This was all what the man had to told me to prepare.

After they checked all my medical paperwork they let me return to the boarding area and we boarded the plane without much of a fuss. The people in the waiting room thought were obviously relieved to see us return. At that time in Iran, everyone was so anxious and fearful that incidents like that could have meant that they were going to search the entire plane.

The plane took off from Tehran and I breathed a heavy sigh of relief. I had no idea what lie ahead in the Netherlands, but was certain it would be better than what we had left. About a half hour into the journey the plane made a small stop in Turkey that I didn't even know was on the agenda. I was concerned and began thinking that they had found out about our plans and were diverting the plane to take us back to Iran. I told MJ not to talk to anyone if they came over to ask him questions. We stopped for 30 minutes or so, and didn't get off the plane. Then without any explanation the plane took off again. I thought for sure they were coming to take us away. I didn't eat or drink anything because I was so worried. MJ was almost 9 years old now. If I nodded my head he could speak, but otherwise he was supposed to act like a mute. He was so very brave. At one moment, he whispered,

"Mom can I talk? I need to go to the bathroom." It was a nerve-racking experience for both of us and the anticipation was killing me. I began to relax as we climbed to a high cruising level and appeared to be on our way to the Netherlands. I was still dressed in the traditional scarf at that point, and after we were certain we were in European airspace all the women on board including myself took off our headscarves.

As soon as we arrived in the Netherlands they held us in custody with the intention to send us back to Iran with the next flight for not each having a Visa. I was told to go straight to the bathroom and flush all my official documents including my passport to truly claim asylum. I didn't do this however; I simply hid my passport and my ticket. They found my ticket. I told them I am here to claim asylum. We went through the customs line and they asked for our visas. This is when I said that we didn't have any. There was an Iranian man there that was a passenger who lived in Canada he helped translate. He said," No you don't want to be a refugee you should turn around and go back to Iran." I explained that my husband and another son were already here. He finally understood our situation and was relieved that I had a husband to go to. He said the refugee situation for single women was horrible. He then helped us say the right things to the authorities, and we were on our way to becoming official refugees.

They took us to a different area of the airport to complete the process and get us assigned to a camp. After a short intake process they had given us until sunset to report to the camp, which was located on the border of Germany and Netherlands. I didn't know the language or my way around the country so I contacted my brother in law and he told me to hang in there and that he would pick us up. About an hour later he arrived. I could hardly believe my eyes when he arrived. I was so relieved that the first most dangerous part of our journey was over.

He was very happy that everything had gone so well so far,

and took us to his house first to be reunited with Amin and Omid. I was overjoyed when I saw them and hugged them both so tightly. However, I could see that Amin had worry painted all over his face. Living in the camp for 4 weeks had changed him and his perspective. He warned me that no matter what happened that he was never going back to Iran, and that I should adjust to our new circumstances and make the best of it. He then described how hard life was at the camp.

"Don't expect any fancy dinners," he said before we left.

My brother-in-law made a few calls and told the authorities that he'd be taking all of us together to the same camp that Amin and Omid had been staying at in Den Haag. On our way to the refugee camp we had a long conversation about the law of the country and all the new positive as well as negative issues we'd encounter in this new country. When we arrived at the camp I realized just how hard our journey was going to be.

My husband and my son Omid were sharing a room with 4 other people and it had about 6 beds. The refugee center was made with a large hall, which was used to serve meals, and as a general area to hang out. There were times I would just sit and observe. I would see some people smoking cigarettes, some taking naps, some playing games and so many kids running around playing tag or trying to jump in the line for meals. It was all very interesting to me. I found myself in disbelief a lot of times, just sitting and asking myself if this was all happening. I would have never imagined that this was our family's future. After a couple of days there they decided to move our family to the camp that I had been assigned to at the airport because of space issues. They gave us a small bit of information and sent us on our way on the train.

It wasn't an easy task to find the refugee center. We had to change several trains and after the last stop we had a long walk because the refugee center was outside of the town in the farm country. Finally, after a full day traveling we arrived. We were tired and hungry but the first thing we had to do was to get all the office work done so we could stay there legally. We reported ourselves to the campus police and after the registration was completed they assigned to us a small camping RV.

The RV was clean, furnished and all the comforts of home were all in their place. It was small, but a great relief after what we had been living in at the center in Den Haag. After checking out our new mobile home they showed us around the points of interest, such as where the showers, bathrooms, cafeteria and the nurse office were. At that moment, I couldn't help but wonder how in the world we'd go to the bathroom at night. It was so far away from our place, and it was quite windy. It was a scary walk to make by yourself. After we put our stuff into our mobile home we went to the cafeteria where there was huge line with all sorts of people from around the world who were waiting to get fed as well.

Amin and I glanced at each other and communicated just by looking at each other. I was so embarrassed to be there, and tears were coming down my face. I asked myself, "What are you doing here standing in a line to get a plate of food?"

There were so many things going through my head. So many stressed thoughts playing repeatedly about how we had no future until suddenly I heard my son’s voice.

MJ said, "Mom I am hungry, I am tired please move up and get some food."

It was a very long day for my kids and all they wanted to do was to eat and get settled in to rest. In my mind our life as refugees started from that night.

CHAPTER 6

The first weeks at our new camp were unlike anything we had ever experienced before. The children were fascinated with every little new thing they found, and would chase the unfamiliar animals around trying to get a good look at them. We would go to the cafeteria several times a day for meals, and this began to feel like a familiar routine making our new life real in a way.

Even with all the hardships that we had faced in Iran, I was not convinced that we had made the right choice for our family. It was an overwhelming situation and I could not see how we could ever make a successful life from our circumstances. These thoughts were for nothing though because I knew that there was no life to go back to in Iran. We'd never be welcome again in our country now that we had claimed political asylum.

Our new life was uncomfortable, but it was also exciting to be living in this new place, and getting to know the culture after talking about it for so long. The worst part for me was that the days passed by slowly because I had very little to do. I was bored out of my mind, and tried to keep myself busy with reading or cleaning the trailer. This would only go so far though, and I longed for human interaction, and began to miss the company of my family back home very much.

Even in my loneliness I was hesitant to make new friends. Amin's brother had warned us not to communicate with any other Iranians in the camp until we had secured our citizenship.

"You never know who these people are," he used to say. "They could be criminals, or spies and really hurt your case for citizenship."

This always seemed strange to me, but I did try to respect this rule as much as I could. However, there were times when I just couldn't help myself. There was a nice family of four from Shiraz that I sometimes spoke to when Amin wasn't around. The young woman's name was Fary, and we were both grateful for the little conversations that were possible between us.

I also kept myself busy by taking walks down into town. The town was so small that you could see everything in about an hour, and I became very well acquainted with the layout and local culture after a few short weeks. I made sure to be back at camp every day before lunch so we could go together to the cafeteria to wait for our food. I noticed that after a while, little by little, my husband Amin started talking with other people too. I could tell he was starting to feel more comfortable in our new home, and this made me feel even more at ease.

The kids had very little problem adjusting. Things were new and exciting for both MJ and Omid. They were always busy exploring or playing around the camp making new friends. The camp even gave us some toys for Omid to play with and MJ loved to bike around the camp and play soccer with the other kids.

Soon after we had arrived they informed us that MJ would have to enroll in school and attend with all the other local children as well as the other refugees. At first he was excited to start school and meet all the new kids, but after his first day he was terrified to go back. He came home very sad with tears in his eyes, and explained that he couldn't understand anything the teacher was saying and couldn't talk with his classmates. Luckily, the camp soon began providing a special tutor to help the children with language skills. This helped MJ feel more comfortable in his new school. I was relieved, and happy to see him start to make new friends there.

Besides these day-to-day activities, there wasn’t much to do but wait. We were told that we would soon be given our first immigration interviews, but we didn't know how long we had to wait until it happened. All we kept hearing was that someone from the immigration office would come and interview us, but no date was ever set. The waiting was the hardest part, and the not knowing soon became painful and frustrating.

Eventually the interviews did begin though after a few weeks. Of course, Amin and his Brother consulted a lot with some of his friends about the proper way to handle the interview. They had created a case for us that detailed all our problems in Iran. Amin and I would have to talk in a way that would be convincing about the issues we were facing so we could get approved by the immigration office.

Finally, that day had arrived and we finally got our interview. Amin and I were terrified beforehand. We knew that everything was riding on this interview and didn't want to mess it up. Amin coached me on my answers to make sure we would answer similarly, and to ease the pressure a little. They asked us so many questions I had never been asked so many questions in my life. After 4 hours of asking questions they told us that we would receive a copy of the interview within 6-8 weeks and if there was anything wrong or was missing to let them know and they will have added into our file.

That was it. After the interview was done, we went back to waiting.

After a few weeks living in the Netherlands as refugees we were getting closer to Norouz, which is the Persian New Year. At that time my mind heart was in my home country with my family and all the rituals they do around the Norouz time. My brother-in-law talked to the manager of the camp and asked if we could go over to their house for Norouz and they approved it. We were so happy to get out of the camp and we felt like we were finally free. The kids especially were very excited and happy. On our way, there we had to change a few trains and one of the transitions I was a little too slow and got stuck on the wrong train. I was so scared because I didn't know what to do, and I didn't know the language or where to go. Some of the passengers saw what happened so they waited with me till the next stop they found the conductor and they explained to him what had happened.

At that time, all I could do was hand the conductor my brother-in-law's phone number. My brother-in-law gave them his address and they helped me all the way to his house with patience and kindness. At every stop, they would pass me to another conductor to make sure I won't get lost again. This kindness was very surprising to me thinking how they could be so nice to someone that they don't know and most of all is a foreigner. In Iran, it would have been unheard of for anyone to help a stranger like that, especially a woman alone.

I finally arrived and we could begin the celebration. My brother-in-law was trying to make it a very pleasant new year for the kids and us. I realized at the time that this was making his wife very upset for some reason. Almost as if she didn't like all the attention our family was getting. I tried not to think about it though because getting out of that camp was enough of a reason for me to celebrate and I wasn't going to let anyone or anything ruin our weekend. That small vacation went by in a flash and before we knew it we had to go back to the camp. The kids were distraught at the thought of going back and cried and cried, but there was nothing we could do and we returned to our secluded home.

We didn't have much time to get back to the boredom of everyday life, however, because just a few short days after our interview we found out that the City Council of Eibergen had voted to close our camp. The local city governments in Holland have an enormous amount of control over what goes on in their districts, and in the case of Eibergen, the locals had become fed up with an increase in crime since the refugee camp had been opened. The local shops also complained about an increase in shoplifting since the refugees had come in. Of course, there was no way to prove exactly who was responsible for this overall increase in crime, but after a few Yugoslavian kids had been caught stealing, the town decided that they wanted all the refugees out.

The camp posted an alert on the bulletin board letting us all know that the camp was going to be shut down, and that we would all be transferred to other camps around Holland. Every day we would all rush to the bulletin board to see if our names had been posted yet with the location of our new camps. After each posting there were people crying as well as others hugging each other and rejoicing because of their new camp assignments. It was an odd situation for me because I didn't know much about the other camps, and wouldn't have known if I had been assigned a good one or not. Over time though we started to hear rumors about certain camps being like prisons, or labor camps, and as more and more people left we got more and more nervous that we might be sent to one of these places. There was nothing we could do about it either way, so again we waited.

The camp was especially eerie at night. The strong winds that would rush across the flat land at night seemed even more intense as they knocked the open doors of empty trailers around repeatedly. It felt like a cemetery with faint whispers of the ghosts that used to be there, and the rest of the living just waiting to hear our final fates.

Finally, the last few days before the camp was set to close we saw our names on the transfer list. It was then that we realized that we had been assigned to one of the prison-like camps that everyone was terrified of. We were in disbelief wondering how we as a family could have been assigned to a place like this. Not knowing what else to do, we immediately called Amin's brother for advice. He too was shocked at our new location assignment. He said that the rumors had been true, and that this camp was one of the worst in the entire country. If we did go there we could expect to live in close quarters with 10 or more people from all over the world, and they didn't make special arrangements for families. He told us that we must fight for a change in our assignment and to tell them of my broken hip to strengthen our case.

We did as he said, and begged the officials to change our new camp assignment. At first no one could be convinced to change our final location, not even Amin's brother could help convince them. However, they could see me standing outside of the room as they spoke to Amin the last time with tears running down my face. They then agreed to have me examined by a doctor to see if my claims of a broken hip were true. The doctor of course confirmed my injuries, and after that they began to trust us. Shortly thereafter we were granted a change in relocation, but were told that we'd have to wait a few days so a room could be prepared for us in a small camp near the city of Rotterdam.

After a few days of waiting we were finally put on a bus and transferred to what was to be our new home in a tiny, beautiful town called Krimpen. The bus pulled up in front of a small hotel and we realized this was to be our new home. It was an older hotel with three stories, and was situated next to a Chinese restaurant. It was quite different from our previous home in Eibergen, and we were anxious to see what our accommodations would be like. First things first, we went to the office and checked ourselves in with the camp officials. After all the paperwork was done they gave us our room key, and we went off to find our room.

It was on the third floor at the end of the hall in a corner. When we walked inside of our room we were very surprised and shocked by the size. The room was just 10 feet by 10 feet, with 2 bunk beds, a table with a small TV, a coffee maker, and four coffee mugs. There was no closet or cabinet for us to put our clothing in because the room was so small. The bathroom and shower were located right by the entry door, which also was very small. This was a luxury though, because at least we'd be able to shower in private now and not have to leave our room to use the toilet.

At that time, we didn't know how long we had to stay in

that small room, but we wanted to make the best of it nonetheless. We took some of our personal items out so we didn't crowd the room even more. The rest of our things we left in the suitcases and placed them under the bed. After we were settled in we went downstairs to explore the area a bit.

The ground level of the hotel was occupied by the cafeteria, a game room and a general lounge where many of the refugees spent time getting to know each other. We met some Iranians there and discovered that there were quite a few other Iranians families living there in the converted hotel.

We first met a young Iranian couple that had come from France. The Husband was a little overweight and he did not like working. He had heard that the Netherlands was a good place to immigrate to because, " If you don't work they will give you a place to stay, and give you a salary to live on," he would say. His wife was only 16 years old and was obviously just trying to follow her new husband. They were roommates with two other Iranians, a middle-aged man by the name of Bijan, and a single lady named Soheila.

If you were part of a couple or single, you were expected to share one of these tiny rooms in the hotel camp. Families of four received the one-bedroom units, while the two bedroom rooms held six people.

We then met two sisters by the names of Azita and Mitra who lived down the hall, and were roommates with two other young girls from Africa. There were also 4 single men in a room, and next to them, a father with his three daughters and one son. The dad was very protective over his daughters. There were times that it seemed like they were in jail and that their father was the Warden.

After speaking with a few of the people we found out that the hotel had been transformed into a refugee camp after it went out of business. The Dutch government had purchased the building to help ease the overflow of refugees coming into the country at the time. The previous owners of the hotel could continue managing it once it became a refugee center. The Union was giving the Government of the Netherlands a lot of money for the refuges but most the time they would not spend a lot of money on the refuges by remodeling the place or doing stuff for the refuges they would keep the most of the funds. The managers were greedy and would do anything to take as much free money from the government as possible.

After a few weeks in Krimpen we were beginning to feel more settled, and more at home. However, Amin was still nervous about getting too close with people at the camp. He would tell me that we didn't know who these people were, and that we could be jeopardizing our status in the country if we became friends with the wrong people. While I understood that we needed to be careful, it was still very hard for me to honor my husband's wishes in this regard. I love talking with new people, and would feel alone and depressed without some sort of adult company. We would argue and fight about this all the time, but I did my best to accommodate Amin's wishes.

This new camp was so different from Eibergen, and was almost impossible to live comfortably just because of the size of our room, but one positive aspect to our new home was the food. The cook at the hotel was from Yugoslavia, and we were lucky to enjoy a delicious meal every night. The first time we went to have dinner in the cafeteria all the tables were taken. Then we saw that a few other Iranians got up and asked us to join them. They were very friendly and respectful, but I could see that Amin was not happy about accepting their offer to sit with them. We had no other choice though, and before Amin could say anything against it, they grabbed my youngest son Omid and placed him on their lap. He wasn't shy at all and his loving personality often brought a lot of attention. They loved MJ too, and went on and on about how respectful he was to his elders. In the end Amin accepted their invitation and we ended up having a very good night with them. We talked and laughed a lot, and learned quite a few interesting things about camp and the surrounding town.

The town of Krimpen we learned was very small and they had opened that camp hoping to bring life into the town and stimulate the economy. The camp did in fact provide a lot of good jobs for locals like nurses, cooks, secretaries and social workers. The local businesses benefited too when the refugees would spend our allowance in the town. We would get 30 Guldens, which is about 15 dollars, a week. The police were even getting busier around the town because a few of the refugees broke many of the laws on a regular basis. Even the newspapers were getting busier with new stories every day and their sales were also going up. It seemed that this town had never witnessed so many immigrants and excitement before.

SECTION 3

CHAPTERS 7 - 12

Adjusting to life as refugees is not easy and we learn about what daily life was like for Sara and her family at various refugee camps. We also learn about several other refugee families that touch their lives along the way, as well as Dutch families that reached out to them.

After several years of cramped living, they are moved to their own apartment home where they try to build a normal life. Their undecided citizenship case continues to be a constant worry however, and the stress of an uncertain future begins to take its toll on the family.

It is during this time that Sara and Amin become close with many Dutch friends from a local church and decide to have Amin baptized in their church in order to try and expedite their citizenship case. This plan backfires though, and they end up having to go into hiding to avoid being deported to a certain death sentence in Iran.

During this time, Sara speaks to an Iranian woman who had converted to Christianity. This meeting sparks a curiosity in her spirit and she begins to study the Christian faith with an open heart.

CHAPTER 7

Life at our new hotel camp in Krimpen was different than life at the old camp. Our quarters were unreasonably tight, but in many ways, we also had more freedom than before. We no longer had to ask permission to leave camp, and generally went about our business around town just like the locals. Every Thursday we would line up to have our cards stamped to receive our weekly allowance of 30 Guilder. Besides that, there wasn't much oversight there, and we began to feel comfortable moving around the community.

Most of the time, especially early on, we spent the weekends with my brother-in-law and his family at their home. It was quite a journey and a process to get there from our camp, but in the beginning, it felt like an adventure. First we took the 98 bus from Krimpen to Rotterdam, then from Rotterdam we would catch the train to Den Haag, and finally from Den Haag we would ride another tram to our destination. As weeks, past, the trip got harder and more painful for everyone especially MJ, which I'll explain shortly.

We continued making the trip for some time, however, and my brother-in-law was a great help to us in those early days. We received a letter concerning our immigration interview a few days after we arrived at the camp in Krimpen, and it was Amin's brother that helped us finalize the statements. He read through all the paperwork and made sure to add things where they needed to be added, and to correct all the facts. We then took everything back to the camp and sent the whole package to the courts and awaited their answer on our immigration status.

It was a long and tedious process, and we tried to fill our time with constructive activities that would help us become more and more at home in our new country. The first task on the list was to learn the Dutch language. Amin was especially committed to learning how to speak Dutch so he could make good relationships with some of the locals. He was even more focused on starting his handyman business up again, and speaking the language was the only way he would be able to grow that business, and provide for our family.

In the Netherlands, the children go to school from 8:30am until 12:00pm before they head home for lunch for an hour. Amin knew that this first part of the day was the perfect time for him to focus on his language studies with minimal distractions. He would drop MJ off at school and come straight home to read language books and listen to tapes until about 9:30. After that he spent time volunteering at different places like the retirement home, around Krimpen because it gave him the opportunity to interact with others and practice his Dutch. Dutch is a very difficult language to learn, but he put in a lot of effort to understand it as fast as he could. Because of his intense study he could learn the language much faster than myself. I also studied at least a couple of hours each day, but was not as fast of a learner as Amin.

I would keep myself busy with cleaning the room, doing laundry, and other family-oriented tasks. Some days the laundry alone would take hours because there were only two sets washers and dryers for the nearly 180 people that lived at the camp. The building was only designed to accommodate 70 in its former life as a hotel, but our camp housed more than double that number on a much more permanent basis. The facilities just couldn't handle the load of people, and all their needs.

It was hard trying to keep two kids in such a small space, so we tried our best to spend as little of our time in the room as possible. It was our home, but it was just for sleeping. It was so small that we couldn't do much else in there but sleep. Instead we spent a lot of time outside and around the camp. This would prove to bring its own set of problems, but it was better than being stuffed in the hotel.

It was around this time that MJ made a new friend at

school named Randy. Randy's father was from Indonesia and his mother, Ellen, was Dutch. From what little I saw of her in the beginning I noticed that she was a very pleasant woman who always dressed very nicely and seemed to be very kind. I was still hesitant to trust anyone in those days though, and even though she seemed very nice, I didn't know her.

One day Amin came back from picking up MJ at school, but he was alone. MJ was not with him. I asked him where MJ was, and he told me that Ellen had asked to take him home for lunch, and he saw no reason why not. I was furious. My son meant everything to me, and I couldn't believe that Amin would be so quick to trust people when he had been the one that was always so cautious when we met new people in the camps.

"I can't believe you would just give our son go with complete strangers?" I asked.

Amin just looked at me confused, "She seemed like a nice lady. What's the problem?"

My stomach was sick the whole day until finally Ellen did bring MJ home safe and sound. Of course, he brought her back to our room when they arrived. I was a bit embarrassed for a woman like her to see our pathetic living environment, but I invited her in nonetheless.

When she entered our room, and saw the conditions, tears began to form in her eyes. She asked us quite directly, "Why is a family of four in such a small room?" With the little language that we knew and with some help from MJ, we told her that it was the only room available, and our situation was very rushed after leaving the other camp so we had no other option.

Ellen was shocked and appalled by this. She was determined to help us get a better living situation, and she marched off to the office right then to see if she could talk some sense into the manager. Of course, Antony, the manager didn't want to listen to anything Ellen had to say, and basically told her to mind her own business. He was a large Dutch man who always seemed to be drunk, and wasn't going to listen to this overly excited woman tell him how to run things at his establishment. Ellen was not affected however, by Antony's attitude and rude behavior. She was relentless in her mission, and figured that she'd wear him down over time. She came back every day for three straight days just to bother him about our living conditions.

Fist she tried to guilt him into helping us. "We are hosts to these people!" She would say, "You are stealing from the Dutch government, and treating these people like animals. You should be ashamed of yourself!"

The second day she tried to use fear, "I know a family of four means a big paycheck for you, and believe me the government is going to hear about how you are taking their money and not providing adequate accommodations!"

Still Antony didn't budge. It was only after Ellen came back on the third day with her research about the international laws and the United Nations' programs to pay refugee centers, that he finally took her threats seriously. She told him that she would not only report him to the UN and the government, but that she'd also make sure the media in Krimpen were alerted to his transgressions. That finally did it, and he begrudgingly agreed to get us into a bigger room. Sure, enough, after five days the new room was ready for us.

After a few months of living in an impossibly small 10x10 space with nothing more than a set of bunk beds, a mattress on the floor, and a tiny nightstand, we finally moved to a bigger room. The new room was on the first floor and was located just across from the office. Antony was a vengeful man, and wasn't going to let us just settle in to our new surroundings comfortably. No, he was determined to make life even more difficult for us as punishment for having Ellen fight for us. I imagined that the new location of our room was not by mistake, and he intended to keep a close watch on us from that point on.

We didn't let him get to us though. Our new room had a closet in it! How could we worry about such things when we had gotten what we needed, and could finally make ourselves a little more at home. It was a small improvement but to us it meant everything. We had no idea how long it would be before we'd move out of that little hotel camp, so every inch of space we could gain was a victory for us.

After that we became very close with Ellen and her family. She would come over and talk to me several times a week in our little room. Even with the bit of extra space we had it was still a hotel room. Our late-night conversations were usually whispered and within earshot of my sleeping kids. I was thankful for her companionship, and felt so lucky to have found a genuine friend, the first one since we had left Iran.

Our families were spending more time together too. We even got to meet Ellen's mother shortly after our move when she came to see our new place. She was a classically Dutch, older woman with a serious attitude and a straight face. Her name was Agate.

Ellen had told us how happy her mother had been when she heard that we were being moved to a more suitable room, but you couldn't tell that when we met her. Her expression was always very serious, and she generally did not let her happiness show on her face. She was a very kind and generous woman though, despite her serious demeanor.

In fact, when she came to see our new place she asked if Amin would accompany her to the shopping mall so she could buy us anything we needed for our new room. Amin did as she requested and went with her to the mall. She wanted to buy us a new refrigerator, more storage for clothing, and just about anything else you can think of. Although we appreciated her generosity, there was no way that we could accept such a large gift. Amin told her thank you, but that he couldn't let her do that. She understood, and came back to the camp with Amin.

Our friendship grew to be very strong over the next few months, and in every situation, we found ourselves in, Agate and Ellen supported us. In addition to sharing our experience and culture, we also learned so much about their family and about the Dutch way of life in general. We learned that even though we all thought we were very different, we were more similar than we knew. One night we learned that Ellen was not Agate's only child, and that Ellen had had a brother who had died in war somewhere near Yugoslavia. I always thought that this might have been one of the reasons she felt so connected to Amin. She also knew that we would understand her pain from this just because of what we had already gone through.

I can firmly say that without them, our lives at the camp would have been very different. They always respected us and gave us more than enough attention and ultimately we felt like a part of their family. They would take care of my kids in every possible way they could, and always looked out for them. Some people at the camp saw the relationship we had with them as threatening. They couldn't understand how someone from that country could love and take care of an immigrant family selflessly. Why did they care? Why were they willing to spend so much of their own money on us even though we couldn't accept their gifts? No, most of the others at the camp began to be suspicious of our relationship with Ellen and her family, and held it against us. They were jealous, and decided that if this Dutch family had accepted us, and then maybe we didn't belong with the others at the refugee camp any more. We were no longer welcomed by most people there.

CHAPTER 8

Days were passing by very past and we did not waste any time getting acclimated in our new country. We took this very seriously and wanted to become good Dutch citizens, so with a serious attitude we began learning the language and studied very hard. We had tons of practice because of the contact we had every day with Ellen and her mother. Our language teachers were impressed after just a few months and thought we were progressing a lot. Amin would go to the library every day to listen to tapes. This would help him with his vocabulary and the pronunciation of the words. Amin was anxious to get to work and feel like a normal person again, and all his language study paid off on that front. One of our friends introduced Amin to a senior home that needed a helper, so he started going there and worked in the kitchen every day. In addition to the social stimulation it also helped him with his language even more. It felt like we had come a long way on our journey to find a new home.

The time was flying by, days, weeks, months and we witnessed a lot of things in the camp and we were always waiting for an answer in regards to our case. After some time, we received another letter from the immigration and found out that they had denied our case, but explained that we could appeal the decision so our case could stay open.

With talking to my brother-in-law again and getting his advice we made a claim for appeal but we didn't know what they would need from us to come to a different conclusion.

We never discussed it with anyone else or asked advice from anyone else in regards to our case besides my brother-in-law. Amin would do everything that his brother told him to do with our case, and we just assumed that things were progressing normally.

Days went by slowly at the hotel just like at the camp before and boredom was always a problem. It was during these times when I had little to fill my time that I would miss home the most. I missed my family and would write letters to them, and assure my mother that all was well. Then some nights Ellen and her mom would come to visit us and the room was so small that we could hear the children breathing while we whispered. I would never forget those nights when that mother and daughter would come with compassion and show us a love and friendship that we had never experienced before. Every time Ellen's mother would come over she would bring the kids all kinds of things just to see the smile on their faces. Even though she had a very serious look on her face, she had a very sweet heart and the attention she gave MJ and Omid was touching. It was like they were her own grandchildren.

At the end of every week we would go over to my brother-in-law's house. In the beginning, it was good but after time his wife became more and more of a problem for us. She would get into our business and the way she treated my kids made me very uncomfortable. She would insult us and talk about us so badly in a backhanded way so it would seem rude if we confronted her.

I would always tell Amin, "Why do we have to go there every week to hear all this nonsense?"

He would always respond by saying that his brother expects us there and that it would be rude not to go. He always put Amin on the spot and at the end of our stay there he would say, "Don't forget to come next week!" I tried to let Amin to by himself, but in the end, I couldn't let him go through it alone. So, we continued, and it only became worse. It was very uncomfortable for us and tortuous for my kids. She treated them like dogs. She'd give them a little bit of food from her hand and make them stay on the couch for hours at a time. She would put out treats like chocolates and hard candies. I told the kids not to touch it because I knew she didn't want us to.

The kids would walk by the table and she would say, "Do you know how much that costs? Don't touch it!"

Amin's older Sister lived there with her children as well close to his brother's house but we did not have any address or phone number from them. My brother-in-law and his wife tried very hard to keep us from their other family. It was all very confusing as to why they acted this way. In the end, I could tell that they were trying to control us for some reason, and over time we realized that we couldn't trust them or anyone to have our best interests at heart.

After we had been in Krimpen for about six months we found out through Amin's brother that his father was very sick. We tried to call him many times but their phone number had been changed and Amin's brother would not give their new number to us. Amin was a very responsible child towards his parents and the entire family. Even as we were having our struggles in the beginning of our marriage I could see Amin's commitment to his family was genuine. The night Amin was at the airport in Iran to come to the Netherlands his father right there at the airport started feeling sick from crying too much and they took him home right away. Ever since then his health wasn't the same and never felt 100% better again.

Then one day my brother-in-law's wife called the camp and said that Amin's father was not well, and that he wanted to say bye to his children. When I heard this, I was heartbroken. I knew that Amin would never forgive himself if he couldn't speak to his father one more time. I asked her to tell me where his father was now and how could we contact him, but she still refused to give me a number. She said that they had talked to him about Amin that his father didn't want to hear Amin's voice at all and that it was all Amin's fault that he got sick after he left Iran and that he would never forgive him.

I didn't know what to say. I knew that this was not my father-in-law's wishes. He had loved Amin so intensely and there was no way this could all be true. I don't know why I didn't tell Amin everything that was said to me. Maybe I didn't want to hurt him any more than I had to. So, I just told him that his father was not doing well. Then after some time we found out the truth and that it had all been a lie, but by then it was too late. When my father-in-law would call, and ask for Amin they would say that they didn't know where he was and that they haven't heard from him in a while. He also asked Amin's older sister to find Amin so he can talk to him one last time. She promised him that whatever it takes or how long it takes she would find Amin for him so he could hear his son's voice one more time. The first step she took to find Amin was to ask her brother of course, and they lied to her and told her they didn't know where we were. It was only when she asked the immigration office later that we would all get in contact with each other. Though it was too late for Amin's father, it was still a relief for us when she found us.

One morning we were sitting in our room and someone was knocking on the door Amin went to open the door and when he opened it his niece and her husband we standing right there and we were so happy to see them.

When we asked them how they found us they explained the whole story. We were in shock by what they told us but we were very happy to be reunited with them.

In those days Amin shed a lot of tears after losing his father and not being able to talk to him on last time. He would sit places and think and not say a word to anyone for days. Nothing could console his grief, and it broke his heart that it was all because of jealousy and petty issues. In the end though things started to improve and we began spending more time with this new part of our family and cut out the ones that meant us harm.

Time continued to go by and we were about to witness our second Christmas in the Netherlands. It was still very new for us and we didn't understand the reason for Christmas or what the story behind it was or why it is on December the 25th. However, we still enjoyed it because of all the excitement that was going on in the city and the joyful Christmas spirit that was everywhere. We just assumed it was a Dutch cultural tradition. I would compare Christmas to the Persian New Year and there were some similarities that I noticed. For example, the time of the year was similar, and people gave gifts at both. I thought the whole thing was very interesting and beautiful.

That year we had a great Christmas even though we were going through a lot and were tired of our living status at the camp. There were times we had to stay in our room for days at a time, but when it was not raining we would go as a family on bike rides to enjoy all the Christmas decorations and lighting. One day we received an invitation from Ellen's mother to go over to her house for a Christmas party and we were so excited to accept the invite. The party was fantastic and she was always very loving to us like a mother. She never treated us like strangers, but as her own family. She had asked the kids what they'd like to eat or what kind of toys they wanted. She even asked MJ about what Amin and I liked. It was such a beautiful and surprise that we could not believe it. That night was so fun and amazing, especially when Amin and I could see our kids being so happy and full of smiles and laughter in the arms of Ellen and her mother. At that moment Amin and I truly realized that we had not seen this kind of joy and laughter from our kids in a very long time. It was truly humbling to see such generosity from our Dutch friends, and was the perfect way to celebrate the end of the year.

At that time, per the law, those who lived more than one year in the camp were eligible to own a house of their own. The law was applicable to us as well but still we had no news about it. 15 months of living at the hotel camp and nothing. We went to our social worker and asked him if he could apply for the housing for us and after that we would go constantly over there to see what the status of our application was. He would tell us that he contacted the housing program and that our name was on the list all we must do is to wait so there would be an opening for us. Every city council had provided some homes in the city for the immigration programs so they could make some extra money. When Ellen's mother found out about that she went and personally applied for us. She would contact the housing department on a regular base and follow up on it she would also mention that we can't be far away from them.

One day when I was in a very bad mood and was extremely tired of all the negativity that went around the camp, I locked myself in our room to be alone. Suddenly I heard a car breaking hard and a when I looked on the other side of the street where the accident had happened I saw my son MJ. I was in complete shock and saw a large group of people running toward him. I don't know how or with what strength, but I ran to the other side of the street to MJ. I couldn't believe what I was looking at when I got to him. I saw a broken bone in his ankle was just hanging out, and I was frozen right where I was standing. I couldn't say a word my knees were all cold and had no strength to stand up. The police came and right after that the paramedics.

All I could hear at that time was him screaming and saying "Mom my leg help me I have a lot of pain". Today when I am writing my story and having a flashback of what happened that day I have a heartache and can see that scene in front of my eyes again. When we arrived at the hospital they did all kinds of test on him and I also mentioned to the doctor that he had a brain hemorrhage.

They took him right away into the surgery room and without putting him to sleep they stated to work on his ankle. The only thing that they gave him was morphine and after the surgery they put a cast on him. He was in such a pain that they would give him shots constantly. After 48 hours, they allowed us to take him back to the camp and they told us that his leg must be in a cast for 45 days. It was a very hard time for a child with a broken leg in a small room and with all the sickness that was going around in the camp. Eventually MJ and Omid ended up getting chicken pox and lice. It was very hard for MJ because of his feet being in the cast and all the itching and pain that was going through his body made it so he couldn't sleep well at night.

When he moaned, and cried from pain at night it burned my heart and made me suffer right along with him. Sometimes he was in such pain that doctors had to come over and give him more medication or shots. Sometimes I found myself so mad at the driver who hit MJ, but we never found out who it was or what had happened exactly. We had never received a police report so there wasn't much else to do but to focus on his recovery. The time that MJ was at home in bed he had lots of visitors, from his friends and especially Ellen and her mother would come daily to visit him. There were times that I would see tears in Ellen's mother's eyes she loves MJ so much. She never came empty handed and she always tried to make him happy or put a smile on his face. Even his teachers from the camp or school would come visit him and try to entertain him.

Everyone was coming to visit my son and wish him well, and the only people that never came were the people who were Farsi speaking. The people from my own country never came because they were afraid they may catch a disease. Amin and I would look after him day and night until finally he got a little better and started going back to school. Omid who was a very nice and quiet boy would times sit in a corner and look at his brother crying from pain and he would see me with tears in my eyes, and he would come to me and hug me very hard and tell me "Mommy I Love you". With those words, I realized that I had not paid any attention to him at all and that all my focus was on MJ. My sweet little Omid even though he was very young and I am the one that needed to show him love, would hold me and hug me and say the most beautiful words in the world. In those days, the psychological pressure of life and all the issues we had with Amin's family was starting to take its toll on us, but through it all Amin and I stayed strong and grew even closer.

We never cast doubt on our loyalty to each other. We tried in any kind of situation and circumstance to live our daily lives and spent time with our kids and to think positive. On sunny days, we would go on a walk or go on a bike ride. It always helped us clear our heads and stay positive. It was on one of these bike rides that bad luck would strike again, however. We got to an area that was very rough road and full of dirt. It was there that I began to lose control of my bike. I hit the brakes too hard and flew off the bike and injured my leg. They took me to the hospital. When the doctors saw, me they said that I had fractured my leg and they had to put it in a cast.

Now Shary had been so helpful to me. She was like a daughter to me, taking care of my kids taking them to school. She loved my younger son Omid very much. Every time I would thank her for the things she was doing for me her answer would be, "Don't mention it because you had been like a mother to me and loved and cared for me so much."

The doctor had said that I had to be resting for 3 weeks and not do anything. I was very lucky that my husband Amin was so patience and supportive. After about 3 weeks the social worker called me to his office and said that he had witnessed the problems and issues that we had gone through at that camp. He said that even the problems that the people from our own country were trying to put on us did not slip past his radar. He then said, "Today I have very good news for you guys. Your name has been called for a home in Delft. It's a popular city that is located between Rotterdam and Den Haag."

After two years of living at the refugee camp, this was the best news I had heard in a long time. I immediately started planning in my mind. We had only three weeks to move to our new home, and we had so much to do before we left. Amin was very sad because he was a volunteer at the senior living home and he had created such a good relationship with the people who were there. Saying goodbye was very hard for him. Despite all the goodbyes and sadness, he always had great memories from that place. We then started to create a list of all the nice and amazing people that had come into our lives there and made sure to get their numbers and addresses so we could keep in contact with them. We were extremely excited about our move and new home but when we saw the tears and the sadness in Ellen's and her mother's eyes we could see it was going to be hard for her too. We were so touched and moved by this.

We had such a great relationship with each other. Ellen had some problems in her marriage and there were times she would leave her big house and come to our little room and we would just talk with each other for hours. Most of the nights after her kids were tucked into bed she would come to our place and have a cup of tea and smoke a cigarette and she would talk and pout out her heart out. Our little room was a place that she could escape to and be peaceful. Her mother was very upset at her son in law and her daughter's life but she was very happy that Ellen had found a place to be herself.

This relationship that we had created had helped Ellen feel better emotionally and she began looking at life differently. She was always thankful for the relationship we had and now that we were leaving it was very hard for them and us. Amin and I would always try to comfort them and say that we would not be that far and that we still can see each other all the time.

MJ's school also found out that we were moving so they threw a huge goodbye party for him. He got so many gifts from his teacher and the students he could barely bring them all home. At the camp, mostly everyone was happy for us and congratulated us. None of the Iranians however, came out to wish us well and it was all because my brother-in-law's wife. She had so many lies about us to all the Iranians at the camp. She even went to our social worker and tried to spread her rumors there.

He called us to his office and asked us if it was all true. We could tell that he had been very sad because he thought we were talking badly about him. We assured him that it was all untrue, and tried to comfort him. We told him how much we appreciated and loved him for all the hard work he had done for us and our family.

Finally, the day arrived for our move. Ellen's mother and her husband were there to help us. Also, Shary and Mehran helped us load all our stuff into the car that Ellen's Mother had provided. We said our goodbyes to everyone at the camp. Ellen was standing quietly next to the car and tears were just flowing down her face. Her mother was also very sad and was trying to hold back her emotions. Our social worker came to us and said a lot of people have left this camp but I have never witnessed so many people that came when they were leaving. There were times that no one would notice that someone had been transferred but you guys have found so many friends in the little time you were here. He was right. We had found amazing friends and built relationships that would last a lifetime.

Just before we were leaving I was sitting in our room for the last time thinking of all the pain and tears that happened there. I was remembering one incident. Once I had heard MJ crying and screaming as he was running to the room. He was in pain saying that a young Somalian man had beaten him up. He had hit MJ so hard in the face that his hand print was still on his cheek. It seemed like that young man was very strong and had no business beating up someone of MJ's age. I was very worried when I saw his face and hoped that nothing had happened to his eardrums. I called the camp doctor to come check him out and the people who witnessed that went and told the social worker. They called the young man to our room and when he came in I saw in his eyes that he had also been crying. The police at the time had arrived and they took him into custody. I don't know why, but I felt that there was something about that young man's eyes that made me feel very badly for him.

After MJ was taken care of by the doctor they immediately

sent the medical report to the police station. I looked at my son and saw the pain that he was in but at the same time I knew that young man did not hit my son for no reason. Something must have happened to make him get so angry. After MJ had calmed down I asked him what had happened and why this young man had hit him. After hearing MJ's story I quickly went to the police station. I got there and asked if I could speak to the person who oversaw that young man's case and they led me to an integration room.

I waited with MJ to see what would happen. There were also some friends of the young man there who were waiting as well. They looked very worried. After waiting about an hour, they finally let us see the officer in charge. The police officer told us to make a written report and after the report had been filled it would take 48 hours to deport the young man back to his country.

I looked at the young man and told him that I knew the situation he was in and I was truly sorry for my son's behavior. However, his actions were unacceptable and that he should never let his anger get out of control like that. I asked both my son and the young man to look each other in the eyes and apologize. I also told the officer that I had no complaint against this young man because my son was rude and disrespectful to him and the got mad but I know both learned a lesson from this incident.

At that moment, I saw tears coming down that young man's face and he shook my hand, hugged MJ and apologized to him. After that incident, we became good friends. Sometimes during the summer, he would come to our room and put a chair outside and we would sit and enjoy a conversation with each other.

The day we left for our new home, he also came to say goodbye. I realized even through bad times and in unusual situations, with forgiveness you can make good friends. We got into the car and the car began moving. I looked back at that camp one more time and remembered all the good and bad things that happened there for those two long years. It was an experience that would shape us for life, and we were grateful to have had it.

CHAPTER 9

After a long wait, nearly two years, we were finally moving on to the next stage in our immigration journey and were finally going to be able to put down roots in our own home. I was overwhelmed with happiness that our family was being given this opportunity to start fresh in our own place and to finally begin feeling like real members of Dutch society, yet my subconscious was racing with worry over the state of our immigration status. It was like standing near the ocean not knowing when the waves would come and swallow you. These negative thoughts were always there in the back of my mind making it impossible to completely relax and settle into our lives. We had so much to be thankful for, yet we still did not know for sure if we'd be allowed to stay in the Netherlands or if we'd be sent back to our country to a certain death sentence. I liked to think getting our new home assignment was a good sign, but nothing was settled, and we'd have to wait for our final answer from the Dutch government.

On the way to our new home I was in such deep thoughts that I hadn't even noticed the time until we arrived in front of a 3-story apartment building and stopped the car. The name of the street had taken my attention right away. It was called Waugenar Street. The apartment complex was shaped like an "L" and it looked as though it had been newly built. When we entered the apartment, I was so pleasantly surprised that everything there seemed neat and clean. The carpet was the only thing that needed cleaning. Compared to the conditions we had been living in, it was an absolute relief to be in such a clean and lovely space.

There was a small hallway that was leading to 3 bedrooms, restroom and shower, and a decent sized family room with leather gray couches and a white round dining table with 4 chairs. The living room was connected to the kitchen as well. The blinds were light blue and some gray.

It was interesting to me to see how they had used these colors in decorating the home. Iranian architecture and design is focused on being as ornate and fancy as possible, whereas the Dutch we much more practical in their tastes. This was going to be our first real home in the Netherlands and it was exciting for me to create a new style of life for our family. Even if it was a simple apartment, we were going to cherish every inch of it and make it our own. The view from our balcony was very beautiful as well, and the entire apartment had a nice open feel. Again, much different to the style of home we had been accustomed to in Iran.

The kitchen had a gas stove and a refrigerator, and to our surprise, the cabinets were already filled with some silverware and utensils. Everything we'd need for four people was there and in its proper place. The bedrooms each had beds with brand new sheets, blankets and pillows neatly laid out. Amin and I were beyond happy because we truly had not known what to expect of our new accommodations. It was a surprise to say the least, and a huge relief as a parent to know that our children would be able to have their own space again. The kids were also shocked and so happy. They were jumping and running around the house like they had just won the lottery.

When Ellen's mother saw how happy we were she wrapped her arms around us and told us how happy she was for us as well. She was overjoyed to see us out of the last camp, and couldn't wait to see us start this new phase of our lives. She had brought a lot of stuff with her like cleaning supplies to help us clean the house, which we started right away but because the house was already to clean it did not take long to complete. She had also brought some food for us to last us a few days and had made a few homemade dishes for us as well. She even began making us coffee! Most surprisingly she did not allow me to touch anything. She wanted us to feel welcomed in our new home and to be able to enjoy it with each other. Her generosity and kind spirit was so touching, and I was truly thankful that we had made such an incredible friend. We could see that she was genuinely happy for us and wanted to make sure we knew she'd still be there if we needed anything.

"Now don't hesitate to call me anytime, with anything," she kept saying. It was incredible to me that she cared so much.

After a few hours helping us get settled and reminiscing, we said our final goodbyes and were left alone in our new home. I would never forget that night. After years of struggle we finally had our home to relax in together as a family. The kids had already claimed their rooms and started decorating them. More than anything for ourselves, Amin and I were just happy to see our kids happy. So, there it began; a new life in a new home and in a new city.

The next day was like the dawn of a new life, and we couldn't wait to check out our new city. Luckily we had more than enough time to look around the city because Ellen's Mother had provided us with enough food to last a few days, so we decided to explore as much as possible.

Delft was a much bigger city than our previous town of Krimpen. There was a good-sized university and it appears the city was made up of many smaller, well-defined neighborhoods. The neighborhood that we lived in was mostly Dutch natives and there were not many foreigners. This didn't bother us however; as we had made such good Dutch friends before that we were excited to meet our new neighbors.

As we explored downtown Delft I noticed that there were many old and newer buildings mixed together Even as the area had been redesigned over the years, the newer buildings were very classic looking. Delft, we'd find out, was known for their historical buildings and rich cultural history. I could tell they took great pride in their city. This historical importance also drew a lot of tourists, and the center of town was very busy with all the people going every which way.

Around the downtown of the city we also found little canals where tourists could rent boats to go around the city and sightsee on the water. There was also an old church there that was clearly one of the main attractions, it was simply called the "Old Church". The architecture was stunning and we were told that it was one of the oldest churches in the Netherlands with many famous people buried there. It sounded strange to us to bury people in a church, sort of like having a cemetery inside. It was true however, and we were told that many important people were entombed there including a few of the past Kings of the Netherlands. On top of their graves was about 3 feet of stone that supported a carved stone statue of the person that was buried there. It was truly fascinating to us. There was also a tiny stairway that all the tourists use to climb to the very top of the church where they could see a view of the entire city. There was also another church right near the old one that was called the "New Church", which was a much more modern building.

In addition to the church, we were so enthralled with the center of the city. It was full of shopping areas that were made up of both new and old buildings. It was a beautiful place that was full of life.

At the end of our street there was a tram station that would run every 15-30 minutes, but most people would use their bicycles to go to work or get around in the city. Our house was in the south end of the city, which was very quiet and peaceful. There was also a new shopping mall by our house and a mosque built by Turkish immigrants.

We could see the entire city in about two to three days, and after that it was time to check in with our social worker. The first thing we had to do was to open a bank account so we would be able to receive our monthly stipend. They also asked us if there were anything missing in the house or if there were any repairs needed so they could take care of it for us. Amin asked them if we could paint the house in our choice of colors and they said yes. So shortly after they gave us the paint and let us paint it ourselves. Also after a few days they had the carpet changed for the entire house because per their health code every time new families come into the homes they need to change the carpets. It was amazing how well they treated us and how they made sure we had everything we needed. After a couple of days, they also gave us bicycles because the cost of riding the bus and the tram was very high and they knew we wouldn't be able to afford it on our stipend.

After all the paperwork, had been filed and we had registered the kids for school, they also told us about a few different colleges in the area that we could register for ourselves. We'd be able to take language and computer skill classes at no charge if we didn't miss more than three classes. Our social worker urged us to take advantage of this opportunity, and of course we did. We were excited to have constructive things to keep us busy. Since we were not able to work for money legally yet, it was a dream to be able to go to school. It would also make it much easier to get jobs once we were approved for permanent status.

All-in-all our move to Delft had been a huge success. Everything felt as though it was falling into place, and I felt like I was going to be able to finally feel at home. Even Amin's niece Maryam (the daughter of his sister) was in steady contact with us always wanting to help. We also kept in touch with many of the people from our life in Krimpen. For a while Shary and Mehran would come over to our house and spend every weekend with us before returning to the camp on Mondays to get their papers stamped. We only had to visit our social worker once a month now that we had been moved to our own place, but we could see that Shary and Mehran were sad every time they had to leave us to go back to that depressing situation. We tried our best to keep their hopes up and to encourage them to stay strong.

We did not however, go out of our way to communicate

with Amin's brother that had helped us so much in the beginning. After all the deception that surrounded the last days of his father's life, we knew that we could no longer trust them, and that they did not have our best interests at heart. We decided to keep our distance from them and to focus on the positive things that were happening in our lives. Amin and I even found that we were getting in less arguments at our new home. Life was getting better, less stressed, and we no longer were so concerned about other peoples' opinions about our lives.

We would take turns taking the kids to school in the mornings and then both go to school ourselves to our Dutch language classes. Our college was far from the house and we had to bike everyday quite a long distance and because of my broken hip from accident I was much slower than Amin. So, he would always leave before me so he could be home when the kids arrived from school.

On one of the many days that Amin left for home earlier than me, a gentleman showed up at our house and introduced himself as Pastor Blenk. He gave Amin an old book that Amin assumed was a historical book about the area as a gift and told him that he had gotten our address from the kid's club that our children used to go on Wednesdays in Krimpen. The people who run it had asked him to check on us in our new home. He also gave Amin a card with an address on it and invited our family to join them on Sunday at 10am. Amin noticed that the address was for a building near the center of Delft. When I arrived home this gentleman had already left the house and Amin told me all about it. Amin seemed to have been impressed with this man and his demeanor and said that he was very nice and so welcoming. I was shocked that we had already had our first Dutch guest at our new home, and we hadn't even had time to make any new friends. It was an unexpected invitation, but we were eager to meet new friends and learn more about our new city.

From the day that gentleman came to our house and gave

us that book it seemed like the road our lives were on changed dramatically. I didn't know how or why he had been placed in our path but he was. Later, I found out that the people who were picking our kids to take them to the kid's club on Wednesdays had approached our social worker and went out of their way to get our new address to Pastor Blenk so the kids would relate to a new club in Delft. The entire time the children were going to that club I just assumed it was a kid's club. I had no idea that it was tied to a religious group, and that it was a Christian-based club. I also had no idea that when Pastor Blenk invited us down to meet up on Sunday that it was for a Christian church service. There were many surprises that would come from this meeting.

We came to this new country with grand plans of what our future would look like, but we soon learned that it is God who has plans for our lives and wants the best for us. Our plans fade away when we embrace the path that God has put us on. Jeremiah 29:11 says, "For I Know the plans I have for you says the Lord they are plans for good and not disaster to give you future and hope." Even at times when we are kicking and screaming trying to make sense of our lives God can give us a hope that is priceless, and pure and set us on the path to fulfill His plans. That is what happened in our lives.

There was nothing that drew me to the old book that Pastor Blenk had given Amin. I was just very happy and excited to read a book in my native language of Farsi, and from a Dutch person no less! It was a kind gesture and I could tell that he had much respect and care for us to go out of his way to bring us a book in our own language.

I have always loved to read, especially when it is a good story. So, when I opened the book and saw the first chapter called "Genesis" and the first line described the beginning of everything including the creation of earth and humanity it made me interested in reading more. Still I had no idea that this was in fact a Bible. I simply thought it was a good historical story. That

Sunday Amin and MJ went to the address that was given to him by Pastor Blenk. It was only then that Amin realized that the meeting place was the Old Church we had admired when we first toured the city of Delft. Even then he thought that it was just a popular historical site that attracted a lot of tourists. The word "church" didn't mean anything to us at that time because we had no prior frame of reference. We were never taught about Christianity at all in our culture, only that we weren't Christian, and that it was illegal to ever become one.

Amin and MJ said that they were confused when they entered the church because everyone was standing quietly in rows and listening to the choir sing with the accompaniment of an old organ. The people then began to follow along and sing while reading from books. After the singing Pastor Blenk appeared at the head of the room and began speaking to the crowd. By this time Amin had realized that this was a Christian religious service and the man that had come to offer us the book was a leader of the church. Pastor Blenk continued and said a blessing over the congregation.

After the blessing, they passed around a bucket to everyone in the crowd. Amin didn't know what the bucket was for. He thought maybe it was like in a mosque when they pour a very nicely scented liquid into your hands. So, he brought his hand forward so they could pour something into them. The gentleman who was passing out the bucket somehow managed to explain with hand gestures that nothing comes out of the bucket but that you must put something in it. Amin was so embarrassed and immediately put his head down. In Islam, there is no collection bucket, but rather every family is required to meet personally with their Mullah each week to give them their monetary offering. So, it was all new to Amin.

They stayed for the entire service that day which was nearly 2 hours. Everyone who was sitting around them could not help but notice them, and look at them quizzically. We were later told that we had been the first foreigners and the first Muslims to ever come to the church for service. As soon as the service was over Pastor Blenk came over to personally welcome Amin and MJ. He was very happy that Amin and MJ had decided to come that day, and while they were talking a crowd of people began to form around them. There were so many members of the church waiting to welcome them and to introduce themselves. A few of the people even got our phone number and address right then and there so they could stop by and visit with us.

I had been eagerly awaiting their return and when they got home they both began telling me about their interesting experience. Amin explained that he had realized that these people were Christians and that this must have been a church service. That was the first experience that any of us had ever had with Christianity, churches, or Christians in general. I was shocked by all of it, but began thinking about why we had never even visited the inside of a church. It was all new for us. We had never even had the freedom to explore these sorts of things before.

After some time, had passed Amin went back to the church again. He would then continue to go back every now and then for quite a while. I joined him a few times purely out of curiosity, but had no inner desire pushing me to explore it much further. Amin got to know a few people there over time though, and eventually invited one of the families to come visit us at our home. One of these families were the Plumps.

One Sunday after the service, the Plumps came to our house. I did not go to church often with Amin and did not know them that well, but their attitude and their kindness was so amazing that it seemed like we had known them for years. That Sunday afternoon we talked a lot, our Dutch was getting better and better and we had a wonderful conversation with them. They had a huge family and their children from their oldest daughter to their youngest child were so kind and loving to us. We became very close friends very quickly. When I told Maryam that we had met this wonderful family and that many others from the church had also invited us to their homes, she said that we were so lucky to have made so many Dutch friends in such a short time. She said that in her experience the Dutch people didn't get close with anyone this quickly especially foreigners. It is understandable how Maryam would see this as good luck, but now that I look back I see that God's hand was over family and He put those amazing people in our path so that we could learn from them.

Things were moving along and we were feeling more and more at home in Delft, but we couldn't shake the uncertainty of our immigration status. No matter what happened with all our friendships, school or family, none of it was permanent if we didn't get that approval to stay from the government. It had been about 6 months since we had moved into our new home and we had still not heard anything from the immigration courts. All together it had been about 2.5 years that we had been living in the Netherlands, and yes we were getting help from the government with our living expenses and other things but still nothing had progressed with our immigration status. It was paralyzing and made it almost impossible to truly feel at ease. We couldn't legally work for our own money, and there were many other things that required proof of citizenship. We couldn't plan our future for our children, and it was beginning to eat away at me.

Finally, after a few more months we received our second denial. It stated that they could not approve our permanent stay in the Netherlands. We were very worried and beyond sad. We couldn't understand why this is happening to us of all people. There were many people from our old camp that had already been approved. Why were we having so much trouble? We decided to visit the immigration office and ask them in person why they had denied us twice.

When we were finally able to speak to an immigration officer and ask him about our case he told us that it was just bad luck. We asked him if it was a lottery-based system to get approved. He then told us, "Yes it's kind of like a lottery. They place a pile of applications on one side of the table and another pile of applications on another side and the judge approves the ones on one side and denies the others. You'll just have to try your luck again."

He saw the shocked look on our faces and laughed. We realized he was just joking. The humor was lost on us that day, but we'd come to cherish this type of typical Dutch dry humor. He was right in one sense though. We did have to try our luck again. So, we again appealed the decision.

CHAPTER 10

Believe it or not after a while I started to believe that in fact it was true that to be approved for citizenship for the Netherlands you had to have a stroke of good luck. From what I witnessed the approval process was not based on merit, political beliefs or connections at all, but was indeed very random. Even if your life was in danger, it didn't seem to have any effect on the likelihood of getting citizenship approval. While many people of questionable character were approved long before we ever had an answer. We talked to Maryam and her husband to see if they had any ideas on how we could get the approval process expedited because the not knowing and the waiting was what was starting to destroy my peace of mind. I needed to have a concrete answer so we could plan our future as a family. what happens tomorrow to you or your kids it wasn't a peaceful life.

Many of our friends didn't understand why it was such a big deal for us to get our approval. They would say things to us like, "You are here and they are paying for you to live here. So, what's the difference between being a citizen and not?"

I tried to explain it to them by saying it was like building your house on a bed of sand, and that with every wind you were worried that all your hard work would be blown away. We wanted to build a better life for our family and contribute to society in our new country, but all of that was delayed because we didn't have our approval. We also saw on the television so many horror stories about how the immigration police would storm in on people simply eating their dinners, totally unannounced and at random. They would storm in and take the family out of their home and deport them back to their home country. It was like living a fugitive's when all we wanted to do was to live peacefully and stop worrying.

When we asked Maryam and her husband for advice they

said that they had heard of people changing their religion from Islam to Christianity, and then had their citizenship application 100% approved. They didn't think they even needed any proof, but to simply declare that they were Christians. They could not return to their country after that because everyone knows that the punishment for converting to Christianity in Iran is death.

Maryam and her husband suggested that we use our connections that we already had with the church in Delft, and pretend to be interested in converting to Christianity. We could then become fake Christians with the help of these people and get them to vouch for us with the courts. We were so tired of living a life of uncertainty, and even though it felt wrong, we decided to consider the rules and decide if we should move forward with this plan.

We did some research and sure enough found out that the punishment in Iran for any Muslim converting to any other religion, including Christianity, is death. Things had gotten even worse since we had left Iran and we knew that if we decided to become fake Christians it would be very dangerous for us if we didn't get our citizenship in the Netherlands. However, after weighing the options we decided that this was the only way we'd be able to get a quick response on our case. It was one of the hardest decisions we ever had to make. I felt as if I was fighting with Allah, and wrestling with the needs of my family. We were not just Islamic in name, but we were still very much trying to live our lives per our religion. I still wasn't convinced that it was the correct way forward, but I trusted Amin's opinion and decided to go along with the plan.

The decision to become "fake Christians" to get our citizenship was difficult but it also reignited our enthusiasm, and gave us something to work towards. Amin threw himself into church headfirst and began attending service every week without fail. We also had heard that he would have to attend special classes to be baptized by the church and that it would take nearly a year before the process was complete. Amin started these classes right away and was determined to never miss one. Even through the bad weather of the Dutch winter, he made sure he made it to every single class. He wanted to show our new friends at the church how serious he was about learning Christianity.

Of course, from the outside it looked as though Amin was ignited by his interest in Christianity, when the truth behind our motivation was very deceptive and felt more and more wrong as time passed. The friends we had become so close to through the church never knew about our lies and what was going on. We were ashamed of ourselves. How could we repay such kindness and love with this type of deception? Today when I am writing this it is the first time that many of our friends in the Netherlands will hear this confession. I pray that now after all this time, the curtain that has been between us and our dear friends will finally be removed. I now know that all of this was part of God's plan to use these wonderful people to bring us to know Christ.

Amin would tell me that every time he was in church or in class he didn't pay attention to the message at all. His mind was fixated on getting his baptism proof, and on nothing else. We knew that if he were successful in becoming a "fake Christian" it could change our lives forever, and that was all we could focus on. Our friends at the church often asked me to come with Amin, but I couldn't bring myself to go on a regular basis. I used my injuries to my hip as an excuse, but I believed that it was a great sin for me to hear the words of this Christian sermon every week. Amin and I continued to practice Islam every day in our home even as we were trying to convince everyone that we wanted to be Christian. I even increased my Islamic rituals because of the immense guilt I was feeling, and though I was appreciative of our new friends' generosity I was having a hard time letting go of certain traditions. We were taught that if you touched a Christian or Jewish person you had to then wash yourself immediately because they were not clean. I was very worried about this while Amin was spending so much time at the church, and I made sure I washed every part of me that touched any of them each night. It is so embarrassing for me to admit now, but it was a part of our culture, and it is never easy to shift your entire belief system. Little, by little we muddled through and were almost entirely focused on Amin's baptism.

During this time, we also continued our studies at the college each day and tried to get good grades so we could show our social worker how seriously we took things. There were people from all over the world in our classes, and there was a nice feeling of friendship between all of us. It was now that we also became friends with a young Persian girl named Rima. She was unlike anyone I had ever met. She was beautiful and seemingly very independent, and was living with her boyfriend without being married. In all my years living in Iran I had never known of a young couple living together without being married. In the Netherlands, this is called "samen wonen", but in Farsi we didn't have a word for it because it simply wasn't done. This was quite a culture shock for me, but as I got to know her I realized what a wonderful person she was, and began to feel sorry for her in many ways.

She was from Northern Iran and had immigrated to the Netherlands after all her siblings had also left the country. She ended up alone in a refugee camp and unfortunately, to escape her loneliness, ended up living with the boyfriend she then had who never truly respected her. Even though things were different culturally in Holland culturally young women, many Iranian refugees had never been taught that they could survive without being dependent on a man. Rima was one of these young women, and she seemed to throw all her trust in whatever young man she was dating at the time. She could get attention from anyone at the drop of a hat, and always presented herself in a very fashionable way. Her family was also very well off in Iran. This combined with her good looks made her an easy tart for men looking for a someone to take advantage of.

One day when she came to class we saw that her faced was covered in bruises. She wasn't acting like herself at all, and during our 15-minute break from class I stopped her to give her our address and told her that she was welcome there any time she needed to come. At that moment, I realized how young and innocent she was. She poured her heart out to me there and began telling me all the problems she was going through with her immigration status, and with her personal life. I told her that we were having a hard time with our immigration process as well, but that we know at least had a hoe of our own, and that she was welcome there. She thanked me and then left. I felt so awful for her. Just knowing that she was all alone in the world and what she must be dealing with because of the bruises on her face. It broke my heart.

A few days after our talk, our doorbell rang very early in the morning. I thought to myself, “Who would ring our doorbell so early in the morning."

When I opened the door, I saw Rima standing there with a bruised face and a with a fountain of tears streaming down her face. As soon as she saw me she threw herself in my arms and started to cry even more, and I noticed she was shivering from being so cold.

I invited her in and poured her a cup of hot tea. I also realized that based on how cold she was, she must have been around the house for at least a few hours before the sunrise just waiting so she could knock on the door. I asked her why she didn't knock on the door sooner. She said that she didn't want to wake us up. I gave the kids breakfast and sent them to school and then told Amin to let our social worker know that I wouldn't be in class that day.

Then the house was completely empty and I could finally could sit down and talk to Rima alone. She finally decided to start talking, and out of nowhere she started to cry even more than before.

My heart ached for and I asked her to calm down and slowly tell me what was going on. She said that she was afraid to tell anyone what had been going on in her personal life, but that she trusted me. After a few minutes, she began telling me her entire story. She had moved to the Netherlands only 18 months before and they had placed her at a refugee camp alone. Many of the Persian people there judged her because of her good looks and thought she was a morally bad woman. During this stay at the camp there was a young man who came often to visit one of his friends and every time he came he would look at Addineh. She could tell that he was very interested in her. She soon found out that he was also from the northern part of Iran and that he already had his citizenship in the Netherlands and was living close by in Delft. That young man gave Addineh his phone number and address and encourage her to call him if she ever needed anything.

She was extremely lonely at the camp and scared of being on her own there. So, one day she called him to see if he would help her get signed up for Dutch classes. He accepted right away and the next morning he showed up to her room and we took her to the social worker's office. She then told me that he asked her to be his girlfriend, and though she was unsure, she decided it was the best decision. It would take her out of the camp and away from all the single men that bothered her there, and possibly help her get her citizenship as well. She had already been denied twice just like us, and she was getting desperate to have things settled.

"I started to get comfortable with him and my feelings toward him grew more every day," she told me. "After a short period he asked me to move in with him. I'd then only have to show up at the camp once a week to get my paper work stamped and get my salary. I accepted his offer right away without even thinking about the consequences that it might bring. It has only been a year since I've been with him, but he has made me feel like I cannot do anything on my own, and has made me afraid of everything and everyone. He doesn't like it when I communicate with anyone else."

Rima was devastated and began to cry loudly in despair. It was clear that he had kicked her out without and hurt her without any regard for where she would go.

"I begged him to wait until morning and to not throw me out in the middle of the night, but he wouldn't listen," she said. "I couldn't go back to the refugee center with bruises on my face so I remembered I had your address and waited until the early morning for a cab to take me here. I was hoping I could stay with you just until the bruises on my face heal? Then I will return to the center and never bother you again."

I felt horrible for her. How could I turn her away? I told her that I would talk to Amin and that we would do whatever we could for her. She had cried so much and it seemed like all physical abuse had made her very tired and weak. It was going to be awhile until Amin and the kids would be home and the house was very quiet at that time. I told her to go in one of the bedrooms and sleep for a bit. Amin came home early that day and I talked to him about Rima and asked him if we could help her out. Amin, who always had a helping heart, also felt devastated for her and agreed that she could stay there with us for if she wanted. He said that his only requirement was that she was not allowed to contact her boyfriend at all.

We tried to explain to her that he didn't love her and that nobody that loves you would treat you that way. We also told her that she needed to be careful from then on. There are many people like this in the refugee center and when they find out about what has happened, who knows? They might try to take advantage of you also or do something even more crazy. The camp was full of people looking to take advantage of a young woman like Rima. The fact that she had money was no secret, and she would have been a great catch for any of them. Many men also made their girlfriends sell their bodies for money. Many of them were on drugs too. No, it was much safer for her to stay with us for now.

She agreed and was extremely happy. Right away we prepared Omid's room for her and we helped her move in all her things. She even offered to pay rent for her room, but we told her that we didn't pay rent ourselves so she shouldn't worry about it either. She stayed with us for months and months, and slowly you could see the happiness come back to her. She was a people person and joked around a lot and was just a joy to have around. We also asked our Dutch friends to help her find a job to keep her busy. So, they helped her find work taking care of a disabled lady three days a week. Rima was a hard-working girl and she would have worked for that lady with all her strength. She was paid under the table of course, because none of us could get official jobs, but it kept her mind off her problems and gave her something to look forward to.

CHAPTER 11

Amin had never gone this long without being able to do the work that he loved doing. He had been a successful handyman in Iran for years, and the stagnation was starting to frustrate him. Not only the frustration of not being able to work toward your family's future, but just the day-to-day activities, or lack thereof were enough to drive him stir crazy. He decided to speak to our social worker about his predicament and the social worker could sympathize with our situation. He offered to bring Amin on as a handyman for the social services. They were always having issues with their buildings and refugee centers, so it would be the perfect place for Amin to feel like he was doing something worthwhile. Of course, he couldn't receive a salary for this work, but that didn't matter to Amin if he could contribute and do the work he loved so much.

The word also spread around our friends at church that Amin was looking for handyman work to do. This eventually led to us meeting a very nice lady named Tiny. She was a very serious woman and very religious. One morning she invited us over for coffee at her house. We began talking and Tiny started asking Amin about his job experience and what he had done for work in Iran. She needed help packing up because she and her husband Cor were going to be moving soon. I quickly suggested that Amin be the one to help. This small task soon turned into regular work for Amin on the side, and Tiny paid him under the table. It wasn't much, but again, it was about being able to contribute that drove Amin.

Working for Tiny was the first independent job that Amin could get in Holland. He continued to find small jobs through our friends, and work consistently after that. He took so much pride in his work that Tiny and our other friends gave Amin a nickname after observing him for a short time; they called him "The Golden

Hands".

Tiny and her husband Cor, also started introducing us to their friends at the church. Like many of the friends we had met in Holland before, they treated us with such respect and love. It was truly amazing to me how we had met such supportive people. After we had been spending quite a bit of time with them they noticed that we were sheltering a young woman who was not technically a member of our family. They respected us for giving so freely to Rima when we ourselves did not know what our future would be. "You are immigrants, and yet you open your doors to another in need." I felt that we were all learning from each other in unexpected ways. It was a truly beautiful time.

Amin was still working hard on all his classes. He was so focused on finishing so he could be baptized that he didn't have much time for anything else, especially now that he had taken on side jobs. However, sometimes at night we'd sit and talk about the Dutch friends we had made at the church and wonder if it was possible for these people to care about us like they did. Though I was thankful for their kindness I was still living with a level of suspicion. There was no way they could care for foreigners like us without wanting something in return. I used to ask Amin if he thought they might have ulterior motives. Maybe they were just being nice to try and convert us to Christianity? Amin was pretending to want to convert, but I was not. Maybe they were trying to brainwash into thinking that Islam wasn't true. I was slowly being drawn into the culture of the church through events with the ladies' groups and it was frightening in many ways.

These suspicions drove me to dwell on very negative things sometimes. I began increasing my practice of the Muslim faith even more out of guilt and fear of what might happen to us. I prayed at all the standard prayer times: morning, afternoon and night. Each time I would get down on my knees and pray to all the prophets of Islam while tears ran down my face. I'd complain about our situation and beg them to help us. Each day I would pray, and each day I only felt worse and worse.

I also watched the television news intently every day. The media in Europe at the time, often made it sound like relations with Iran were better than they were. The UN always chastised Iran in the news because of the horrible human rights violations, but European countries tried to get away with as much as possible to their own benefit. Back door deals and under the table agreements. All because of cheap oil and cheap labor. In the end, it was the people that suffered, the immigrants in particular. Each news story we heard, we thought it could affect our situation. We felt like these stories always got our hopes up for a positive resolution to our situation, only to be let down.

There were also powerful groups within the refugee camps called the "Mojahedin" that preyed on vulnerable refugees. They would wait until they saw that people were denied permanent citizenship and then offer to help them. It was a trap of course, but many refugees had no idea what was going on, or who these people were. They would offer them gifts like tickets to see popular Iranian singers, and gain their trust. Then they would tell them that if they become a member of the Mojahedin they would get their citizenship quickly. The group would force them to commit crimes or even acts of terrorism. Once someone had joined there was no hope for them. There was no way out. The Dutch government could do little to help them, and the Mojahedin themselves made it impossible to leave. They were basically like the mafia of radical Islam and they knew that the refugees were easy targets, and that they could use them without much consequence.

We had even been approached by the Mojahedin before we moved to our home in Delft. They were trying to convince us that they could help us get our citizenship. Luckily Amin and I had seen a Dutch documentary about the group and knew to stay far away from them, but most were not that lucky.

During this time, I also received some devastating news

from home. My mother had become very sick and she had severe pain from her bones. She could no longer walk or do anything anymore and had to be in bed always. My mother loved me in a different way than all my siblings. Even though she tried to hide it her feelings and love toward me often caused jealousy between me and my brothers and sisters. It had been less noticeable before I was married, but once I moved into my own home she was always spending as much time at my house as possible. Then once I had MJ she was there all of them time, and absolutely loved him. He was her last grandchild and because he was my son held a special place in her heart. After we left Iran she became very depressed, and she struggled to stay happy from that time on. This negative thinking, I believe, also contributed to her health issues. She didn't have any joy to look forward to in her life.

I called her as often as possible, and every time I we'd talk I would ask her how she was feeling. Her response was always, "If you were here I wouldn't have gotten sick. Being away from you is like death to me."

She had been sick at times even when I was in Iran, and I would always find time to visit her. My father claimed that she felt better the second she heard my voice on the intercom. Thinking about those times, and realizing now how sick she had become broke my heart. I felt so powerless to fix anything. I told my mother each time on the phone to pray for us to get our citizenship quickly so I could bring her to live with us.

Shortly after her health started to decline my sister told me that the doctors were confused as to why she was in so much pain, and that they were planning on running more extensive testing to find out what was causing her condition. Sure, enough, a few days later they told me that her tests had come back positive for bone cancer.

CHAPTER 12

The situation with my mother's health made the fight for our citizenship even more dire. Our dear friends at the church began trying everything they could to help move our case along. One of the members of the church was also the director of a newspaper, and he began telling our story to all the media outlets. Radio, television, and print; all of them came to interview us about our situation. They were shocked that a family like ours had been denied so many times. It was overwhelming for me. I had never had people make such a big deal over me before, and had never seen so many strangers reach out to show their support to me.

Even with all this attention, our case seemed stalled with no answers. I felt like a coward for not having the guts to just go back to Iran to see my mother. I knew it wasn't practical, and that my children needed me to stay with them, but time was running out and I felt desperate. Our Dutch friends even tried to send an invitation for my mother on their behalf, but with no luck. Our only hope was still to get Amin's baptism finished so we could try to use that as a reason to expedite our approval.

The day of Amin's fake baptism did finally arrive, and we were anxious to get it all over with. I will never forget how our friends at the church were so happy and excited about it. I didn't understand why one person changing their religion was cause for such happiness. At the time, I had no clue about salvation, and the meaning of it all. All I could think about was getting that proof so we could take it to the courts.

Amin had to make a proclamation in front of everyone that he believed in Jesus Christ and that he was turning away from Islam. I knew in my heart that it was all a lie and would be a horrible scandal if anyone ever found out about our true motives. We sat and listened to the rest of the service. The Pastor was preaching about how God has called everyone from every nation, and he quoted John 3:16, "How God so loved the world that he gave his only begotten son that whoever believes in him shall not perish but have eternal life." That day was the first time a Muslim had been baptized in the history of their church and it was an honor for all of them to be a witness to it.

Today when I think about that day I should have taken that opportunity to listen with my heart but unfortunately I didn't. It was as if I was a wolf on a hunting mission with no ability to see anything but the end goal. We had done whatever we had to do to reach this goal, including lying to our friends that cared so deeply for us. Per the Islamic religion, however, our lie could be forgiven because it was for a greater good. Literally translated, this type of lie is called a "fake truth". At least this is how we justified it to ourselves.

After the service, all the members had lined up to hug and congratulate Amin. Maryam and myself were standing next to him as well and looking at the scene of people just looking at each other. Even without words I could tell we were thinking the same thing, "First they brainwash you into becoming a Christian and then they get all happy and want to celebrate your brainwashing!"

It was an odd mix of feelings for me. On one hand, I cared for these people, and on the other, I could never imagine myself ever being anything but a Muslim woman. In our culture, we only ever saw Armenians as Christians and some of the people who were fanatic Muslim called them Kafar (infidel), or unrighteous and filthy. If you were born Armenian, you could be Christian because of your heritage but it is illegal for a Muslim to convert. They are only allowed to hold religious services in their own language, and are strictly prohibited from evangelizing. If an Armenian would go to grocery store and the people who worked there knew they were there, they were not allowed to serve them. They would also throw away anything they had touched because they were considered filthy. That day after Amin's baptism, Morgan and I joked to each other, "Good Amin is an Armenian now."

Shortly after the ceremony they gave us a few papers that certified that Amin had been baptized in the church. I took it in my hands and was overcome with joy. We believed that this one piece of paper was the solution to all our problems, and that we'd now get to live happily ever after with our immigration case settled.

We were all so excited to finally have the paperwork, but I still had a very bad feeling in my spirit and was afraid that I would be punished by Allah for helping Amin become a "fake Christian". It is well known that in Islam it is believed that anyone who turns away from the religion converts to another becomes unholy, and their blood is the filthiest of filthy. When a Muslim child is born the elder in the family whispers "Ashad" into the baby's ear. This is almost like a prayer or testimony that says that Allah is big, Allah is holy and that Mohammed is the last true prophet of Allah. Even though the child cannot understand the words that are being spoken, this is its official invitation into Islam, and from that moment this child can never explore or consider other religions without turning its back on Islam. If that child, or any person born a Muslim decides to convert to another religion, this person can then be justly executed in the name of Islam.

I knew that Amin's conversion wasn't sincere, but was still worried that we had offended Allah with our actions.

We were talking about the baptism on the way home from church that day and decided that we had to do something to make sure we weren't going to be cursed. So, the first thing Amin did when we walked through the door was to have Maryam's husband say the Ashad prayer into his ear as if he were a little child. He also said the forgiveness prayer two times himself. After that we began to feel better. We had gotten our paperwork and successfully voided all of transgressions against Islam. Things were only going to get better from here. Now it was time to wait for our next court date.

Our court date did arrive shortly after Amin's baptism, and we were so confident that everything was going to go great. It was our third appeal by then, and now we had Amin's conversion to support us. We also brought two members of the church to court with us to vouch for our story. We submitted all the paperwork and waited to speak with the judge.

When it was our turn to go before the judge, he reviews our papers and looked at us. In a calm tone, he asked us, "Did you know that the penalty for converting to Christianity is death in your country?"

We answered him humbly and told him that, yes we were aware of the penalty for converting.

"You knew that your case had been denied three times, and there was a good possibility that you may be sent back to your country, and yet you still decided to convert to Christianity?"

We nodded, yes.

"Frankly this has no bearing on the decision to grant you permanent status or not. The fact that you chose to be baptized in a church, while knowing the possible consequence, is not the Dutch Government's problem."

We were in shock, and just stood listening to what else he had to say.

"You came here today hoping for a final decision in your case and thought that this baptism paper would somehow secure your citizenship, but unfortunately that is not the case. Anyone can decide to change their religion in a heartbeat if they think it will prevent them from being deported. No, you'll just have to go back home and wait for the final decision from the immigration office in a few weeks."

Tiny's husband, Cor was there and asked to speak on behalf of the church but the judge denied him permission to speak, and repeated what he had said earlier.

"They'll just have to wait for the final decision, and nothing you say or do will change this."

It was as if the entire world had fallen around us, and we didn't know what to do next. We packed up our things and headed home. The members of the church that were there with us tried to be encouraging, but with the way the judge was acting, we had little hope for a positive decision.

In the days that followed our friends at the church didn't sit still. Even though we had lost all our hope, they only pushed harder. They went out and found us the best immigration lawyer they could and hired them with help from the church funds. I put all my trust in them and just did exactly what they told me to do. It was as if I was a robot, listening and reacting to their words, but with no emotion on the inside. My brain felt foggy and as if it wasn't working at all. I began to obsess about all the bad things we had done, and became convinced that Allah was punishing us. I thought about it constantly, 1000 times a day or more.

I thought maybe this was all happening because I had gotten so far away from Allah with my own selfish desires. So, I decided to pray and fast even more then before so maybe Allah would have mercy on us and forgive us. However, the more I fasted and prayed, the worse I felt. It was a vicious cycle and I started to fall deeper and deeper into despair because nothing seemed to make me feel better. I started smoking cigarettes constantly and just complaining about our situation to anyone and everyone that would listen.

I started to get angry with Allah and blame him for our situation, but didn't know of any other way to get peace other than prayer so I continued to pray to Allah even though I was angry. I would mindlessly repeat my prayers in Arabic that I didn't even understand. My mind would wander and I'd forget how many times I had said a certain prayer so I'd have to start all over again. I was supposed to say each one 17 times several times a day, but sometimes I said extra prayers just to make sure I had done the proper amount. It was so frustrating praying in a language that I didn't understand. I felt no connection to this higher power, Allah at all. I longed for a connection with God, just something that would give me a small light of hope in the darkness I was living in.

It was right around this time that we heard news from Iran that a famous Armenian Pastor named Hayk had been kidnapped by the Republic of Islam in broad daylight right in front of his house. He was then tortured to death and stabbed repeatedly. He wasn't killed because he had born a Christian. He was killed because he had been very outspoken in his support of another man named Mehdi Dibaj, who was a Muslim born man that had publicly converted to Christianity. We also heard that Mehdi Dibaj was arrested but later released. Then a few days later we heard that they had killed him too. He was hung from a tree on a quiet street so no one would know about it until it was over.

We were all shocked by this news. We all knew that you could be killed for converting to Christianity, but we had never heard of it happening to someone, and especially in such a public way. It was clear that the government in Iran had become even more radical since we left, and there was no way that we'd ever receive mercy for what we had done if we were sent back there. It would be nearly impossible to convince them that Amin's conversion had not been real, and we'd have to suffer the consequences as a family if we didn't receive our citizenship.

With everything that was going on it is a wonder that we managed to keep it all going, but we did, and continued to go to school at the university every day and Amin kept working his side jobs. It was during this waiting period that I met two young Iranian women named Marjan and Sara. They happened to live very close to us, and began biking to school with us. They were waiting for their citizenship decisions as well, but seemed so full of hope about the whole thing.

One day Marjan began telling me that she sympathized with me very much, and that she too used to be depressed. She said that she had become depressed while living in one of the refugee camps and that her social worker had moved her to a private home like ours with her two other female roommates. It was then that she met a group of Iranian Christians that lived in the south part of the country. They invited her to their prayer nights and she began attending them without much expectation or interest in Christianity. One night while she was telling the group about her situation she began to cry uncontrollably and the group laid hands on her and prayed for the spirit of depression to leave her. She said when it was over she felt a wonderful, warm feeling through her entire body. She was so moved that right then and there she decided to accept Christ and become a believer. She told me that ever since that day she has had a sort of happiness that she'd never had before. She was still waiting for her immigration case to be settled, but no she knows that God is in control and she had turned her burden over to Him.

While Marjan was giving her testimony, I was all ears. It was very interesting to me to hear how someone born a Muslim had become a follower of Jesus Christ. It was the first time I had ever personally met someone like this. I envied her peaceful state of mind, and wondered if it could be true. Could becoming a Christian help me release the burden of depression and give me the hope I was looking for?

I went home that day and immediately picked up the old book that Pastor Blenk had given to us, and that had been lying on the bookshelf for two years. I started to read the book and study it little by little. Even when Amin had been going to his baptism classes, I had not learned anything about the Bible. Amin never discussed any of it with me. I didn't even know that there was an

Old Testament and a New Testament, or why it was this way. I was starting from scratch, so I began asking Marjan questions here or there hoping she wouldn't notice my interest in it. She was always very kind and would talk to me with excitement about my questions. Maybe she even knew what she was doing, and was secretly encouraging me to keep reading the Bible.

One Saturday morning that fall we received a phone call from the police station telling us that two young women had been in an accident and that the only number they could find on them was ours. We rushed to the hospital and found Marjan and Sara all bruised up from the accident. They had been knocked unconscious initially but luckily would recover with the right care. They didn't have any family that could look after them so Amin and I offered to have them stay with us for a while. We collected their things and brought them home, and got them settled into one of the kids' bedrooms.

They had very deep cuts on their faces and a nurse came every day to change their bandages. Even their mouths had deep cuts on them so they could barely talk. I made them liquid food and would feed one of them with a teaspoon while Amin fed the other at the same time. A few days passed and I asked Marjan for the phone number of her Christian friends in Almere so I could call them and tell them what had happened. We had a warm conversation and they were very thankful that we kept them in the loop and that we were taking good care of Marjan and Sarah. Their tone of voice seemed very nice and peaceful to me, and was not what I would expect from complete strangers. I asked Marjan if they knew me.

She said yes, of course they know you very well. I asked her how this was possible. I thought initially they knew us from our interviews with the news or something related to our case. She then explained that since the first day she met me at college she had told them about our situation, and that they had been praying for our salvation. She said they knew that God had big plans for our lives.

My first reaction was to tell her about Amin's baptism and let her know that they didn't need to pray for our salvation because we had already spent a lot of time in church and know a lot about Christianity. Of course, this was all a lie. Everything the Pastor had said while I was in church didn't sink in, and I had spent all that time asking Allah to forgive me for committing this horrible sin of listening to the Christian sermons. I wanted to make sure though that she knew that she and her friends didn't need to waste their time on me. I already knew about Christianity and was never going to convert.

That's what I wanted to say. That's what I had trained myself to think, but I didn't. When Marjan was talking to me about the power of prayer and the love of God something inside of my spirit was stirring and telling me to listen to her.

As she was finishing her story, she then told me that everything she had to share with me she already had. "Now it's your turn and it's in your hands. I have shared how God has changed my life. Now what are your thoughts about that?"

I burst out with a concern that I had been thinking about for a while, "So you're saying that my parents, and family that were all born Muslims are all going to hell because they don't believe in Jesus Christ and the Bible? Jesus paved the way for the last prophet that is Mohammed. If this were not true, then everyone would have just stayed Christian. So, all of us got it wrong and are now going to hell?"

Marjan looked lovingly at me and responded, "Anyone who has heard the good news of Christ will be judged one day by God. I am not the judge. Today you have heard the good news though, and it's all up to you whether or not to accept it."

I sat in silence. I felt like she was putting even more weight on my shoulders by telling me all of this. "I wish you had never told me."

She smiled and thought I was joking.

"Why are you smiling," I asked.

"Today I have not thrown any seeds on barren ground. No, I have planted good seeds in good soil, and with your words you've shown me that something in you is awake and God has touched your heart."

SECTION 4

CHAPTERS 13 - 15

After these seeds of curiosity for Christianity are planted, they grow through Sara and Amin's quest for righteousness and the truth. Throughout these chapters, we explore many comparisons between what Sara learned growing up in Islam and what she was now learning from her Christian teachers. Her quest leads her to study not only the two faith's holy books, but also look at historical accounts as well.

After much study, searching and prayer, Sara and Amin both have a miraculous conversion experience right on the edge of what could have been their family's darkest moments.

CHAPTER 13

I was left in shock after our conversation about Christianity. I was intrigued, but also very uneasy about the whole thing. Marian and Sarah still had quite a bit of time left in their recovery process, and I knew that this subject was likely to come up again. One day not too long after our conversation, Marjan told me that her Christian friends from Almere, the ones that had praying for me, wanted to come over to check-in on her at our house. I of course agreed. I loved meeting new people anyway, but these people were of interest to me. I was finally going to meet the people that had influenced Marjan's life so dramatically, and had been praying for me and my family. Marian said that they were worried they might not be welcome because of their religion, but I assured them that they were welcome in our home. I was excited to finally meet these Iranian Christians that I had heard so much about.

They came one late afternoon to our home, three of them, with huge smiles on their faces, and joy in their hearts. I was struck by how happy and appreciative they seemed. The one man's name was Farshid. They thanked Amin and me for taking care of Marjan after her accident and brought a beautiful bouquet to show their appreciation. We all sat down and got to know each other a bit through small talk and casual conversation. They wanted to know how I had met Marjan, and asked about our journey to the Netherlands. We also learned that they both were both former refugees and had met while attending university in Amsterdam for computer engineering. They had received their citizenship and had only recently married. Our conversation came very easily and after just a short conversation we felt as if we had known them for years.

Slowly they started to talk about their Christian faith and their beliefs. Farshid was the Pastor of an Iranian church in

Almere, and he shared a little of what the congregation was like. Per the Persian culture, we are required to be very hospitable to every guest we invite into our home regardless of whether or not we agree with them. This meant that we must respectfully listen to everything they had to say. It was very interesting to us because we were hearing these Christian beliefs from people who were born Muslim. They were so confident in these beliefs and this switch to Christianity had clearly brought them huge amount of joy into their hearts. It was a strange and exciting experience just to be able to hear their story.

After they were finished talking about the church and their belief in Christ, Farshid turned to us and said, "God loves you guys very much and he wants the best for you. You must come and experience a taste of this love yourself. You can't compare God's love to anything even to the love of parents for their children. It's a much deeper love and it doesn't have any rules or regulations, but is truly unconditional and all-encompassing."

We had never heard of this concept before. The idea that there is a God that loves us more than our own parents? Up until that point in my life I had been taught to fear Allah, and that Allah knows every mistake I've ever made, and that I'm not worthy of him. The notion that this Christian God loved me was truly mind blowing, and it was something that stuck in my brain and made me want to learn more.

Before they left they asked us if they could pray for us. We said yes, but weren't quite sure what to expect. First we thought that they were going to read a prayer out of a book like we had done in Islam, but it was not like this at all. Instead it was very simple, and they raised their hands toward heaven and started to give thanks to God and asked for blessings upon our house and for everyone inside of our house. Then at the end they said, "In the name of Jesus Christ, amen."

We had seen many people pray at church in Delft before. We had even had them pray for us before, but for some reason this time was different. Maybe it was because it was said in our own language and came from Iranian people, or maybe it was just because we had not been open to it before. For whatever reason this time the prayer moved our souls. It was as if we had eyes before but had been unable to see, and that we had ears but had not been able to hear.

That day Amin and I were truly in awe. Their words, their actions, and especially their prayer had touched us very much. We were also so touched by the sincere love that they had in their hearts. We were fascinated with the fact that we had met these people who were just like us, Iranian refugees and Christians. It was not just for western people, but that Christianity could b for all the people of the world. We had seen Dutch Christians for two years, but after meeting them it was different. A light went on in our hearts.

From that day on, even long after Marjan and Sara had fully recovered and left our house, Amin and I continued to talk about our experience with Farshid and His wife. We also began looking at our friends from the church in Delft in a different way. We realized that they had not been trying to brainwash us into leaving our religion at all, but that it was God's love, Christ's love that was living inside of them that made them genuinely care about us. We had built important and meaningful relationships with our friends from the Delft church before, but the understanding that we gained that day made us understand just how lucky we were to have these amazingly generous and loving people in our lives. We felt very guilty for if our friends had been motivated by something else other than love, but were grateful that we had finally realized the truth. There is a saying in Farsi that loosely translated means, "A friendly wolf always has a secret plan for you." This was the suspicious way in which we had viewed our relationships before, but it was all a part of God's plan for our lives and little by little we were learning that.

Shortly after our conversation Farshid had stopped by to

give us a movie called "The Life of Christ" that had been translated into Farsi. He also brought us a new translation of the Book of Luke. Our curiosity had been piqued after the conversation with Farshid and His wife, but we were still operating out of fear and truthfully we were afraid to watch the movie initially. We were afraid of it being a sin to even watch it, but also afraid of what other questions it might bring up in our hearts. If we allowed ourselves to explore these questions, what else could it lead to? It was a very inspiring but confusing time for Amin and me. Eventually curiosity did get the better of us and we decided to watch the movie. Once we watched it once we were so touched that we decided to watch it a second time that same night! During the second time, we watched it Amin and I both had tears streaming down our faces as we watched. Sure, enough those questions we had been afraid of started plaguing our hearts and minds, and a desire to study the Bible to learn more was ignited in both of us.

After that we decided to attend some of the small groups from the church we went to in Delft so we could study the bible and ask many of the questions we had. When they would talk about the Old Testament and the promises that God had made to Abraham through Isaac I had a hard time believing any of it because it was in complete contradiction to what the Koran had said about the very same events. I was absolutely confused by this. Per the Islamic point of view we too were descended from Abraham through his son Ishmael. The main difference in beliefs came from the fact that the Koran states that Ishmael was the promised child of Abraham not Isaac. In the Muslim tradition Ishmael and his mother Hagar were sent away by God to the desert after they were Abraham banned them from his house just like the Old Testament states. However, once they are in the dessert the story in the Koran becomes different. While Hagar was searching for water to quench her thirsty child, Ishmael began stomping his foot on the ground crying for water. Suddenly on that spot in the ground water began to erupt. The water was called "zamzam", which means heavenly water and it is on that very spot that the Muslims built "The Home of God" which is known now as Mecca.

Every time I listened to these stories I tried to compare what I had learned growing up in the Muslim faith to what I was learning in the church. These differences in doctrine weighed heavy on my mind and I always asked many questions about these points.

One day one of the people from the small group asked me a question. He said, "Who do you think came first Christ or Mohammad?"

I answered him with confidence and said, "Of course Christ came first, but Mohammad came last to finish God's Promises."

Then he asked me, "Do you think The Old Testament and the New Testament came first or the Koran?"

Again, I told him, "Of course first came the Old Testament and then the New Testament and the last Holy book was the Koran."

He asked, "What kind of book do you think the Old and the New Testament are per the Islamic religion?"

I told him that we consider these books to be among all the Holy books, and a smile spread across his face.

He said, "OK then per your own beliefs would there be any lies in any Holy books?"

I answered, "Of course not."

He replied, "So if there couldn't be any lies in any Holy books, how could the Old and New Testaments be wrong? The Old Testament was written a 1000 years or more before the Koran and it teaches that Isaac was the promised son of Abraham, and that it was through Isaac that God's blessings for the nation of

Israel would be fulfilled."

I had sat and quietly thought about what he was saying.

"So how is it possible that God changed his original word? God is not human and does not make mistakes or mislead His children. So why would He send a final prophet named Mohammed 600 years later to show the world that He had been wrong, and that Ishmael was actually the promised son of Abraham?"

I still sat silently listening as he finished. "God always keeps His promises and reveals his truths in His word. Think about what I've said and pray to God to reveal His truth to you."

Later we would learn that the New Testament also predicts that there would be many false prophets after Jesus. One of the many references is in Matthew 24:24, **"For false messiahs and false prophets will appear and perform great signs and wonders to deceive, if possible, even the elect."**

After we left that bible study Amin and I had many doubts and questions about how all of this were possibly true. We'd talk for hours about what all of it could mean, and why it could be true or false. I had been raised since childhood in Islam and had never even considered the idea that it could all be wrong. Amin himself had studied the Koran intensely, memorizing it cover to cover and became a teacher at the Mosque for a time. How could we believe that all those beliefs had been incorrect? These nightly talks that we'd have spurred an even deeper desire to learn about the Bible, and the history of the Christian religion as well as the history of Islam.

We started to study very seriously and began to find other remarkable differences between what the Bible taught and what was in the Koran. For instance, geography wise, the Koran places the desert that Hagar traveled with Ishmael in a totally different area than the Bible does. This was just one of the many differences that we found as we studied. These little differences began to create cracks in my beliefs, the beliefs that had been ingrained in me since I was a child. I came to a place in my mind where I didn’t want to be a Muslim anymore. I wasn't sure I wanted to be a Christian yet either, but I realized that I was Muslim because I was born into a Muslim family and that it was culture, not true knowledge of the religion that made me Muslim. I couldn't accept this anymore after learning what I had learned. I wanted to have the freedom to learn about a religion and make a choice that was true in my heart and soul about my faith. When I was born, my faith had been decided for me through the Ashad prayer, but now I was ready to decide for myself.

During this time, I felt like every direction I turned I saw examples of God's love. In the way, our friends at the church treated us respectfully and always answered our questions, and in their generosity of spirit in so many ways. I related everything I saw of God's love to how Christ embodied that with his life, death and resurrection. It stood out to me that these people were trying to be Christ like. That was one of the most incredible things about Jesus to me, his capacity for love. Again, we had been taught that Jesus was a prophet, but nothing more. I knew nothing about his life, and of course had never heard of his crucifixion and resurrection before we started studying the Bible. One of the most moving stories in the New Testament to me was when Jesus was hanging on the cross and asked God to forgive the very people that had put him there. He had been tortured beyond all belief and instead of revenge or resentment, he had forgiveness and love in his heart. It was incredible and inspiring to me.

I was truly getting to know Christ on a personal level and feel a connection that was unlike anything I had ever experienced in Islam. His example that he had set for his followers was completely different from the prophet I grew up knowing in Mohammed. Mohammed was a leader that waged war on his enemies and spread the religion of Islam through violence and savagery. His children and grandchildren (the prophets of Islam) also spread the religion this way. In fact, Iran only became a Muslim country after a bloody war was waged by one of his grandsons against the Persian Empire.

There was another story in the Koran that stood out to me as being the exact opposite of what Jesus preached. The involves Imam Ali who was Mohammed's son-in-law, and supposedly the first young male to accept Islam. He later became a leader in Islam and was ultimately killed after an assassin hit him with one blow from a poisoned sword while he was praying in a mosque. He died two days later, but told his sons that he wanted to make sure that his assassin was only given the exact equal punishment to his crime, meaning he was to be struck once with a poisoned sword. This was a great mercy.

I thought a lot about that story. I also compared it to how Jesus behaved on the Cross. I could feel the truth in the pit of my stomach, and it kept me up at night.

I also thought about other things that I had been taught in Islam like the Holy month of Ramadan. All Muslims are expected to fast during the day for the entire month of Ramadan. Even as a child I was expected to do this. Many people would also observe strange traditions during this time like sitting in a room with the Koran on their heads while beating themselves on the chest. All of this because it is believed that during this month Allah's blessings are more abundant, and it is considered the month in which the Koran was revealed to Mohammed. It had seemed strange when I was living as a Muslim, but after all my study of Christianity it seemed crazy.

When these questions and new discoveries kept me up at night, I would get up and read the Bible some more. Let me also explain that I wasn't just reading the Bible. I was studying it very deeply and comparing it to Islam word-for-word. I was learning how to speak to God with my own simple words. I didn't need anyone else to talk to God for me. It was a liberating feeling, and I prayed to God to ask Him to reveal the truth to me so I could finally be saved from this confusing I still carried in my brain.

With all our attention focused on our spiritual journey it is a wonder that we had time for anything else in life, but our daily lives continued much as it had before. The gravity of our situation was difficult not to focus on, but we tried very hard not to let those depressed feelings get the better of us. We spent as much time as we could with the kids after school and always tried to keep things upbeat for them. We didn't want them to have to worry about being deported back to Iran, and what consequences might come with that. Though we did try and shield them from this, there were times when we couldn't keep it a secret.

The church and our friends were continually trying to bring attention to our case through the media, and there were often journalists at our house when the kids would get home. Refugees were a hot topic in the media at that time, and everyone was interested in getting to the truth about what was going on between Iran and the Netherlands. The government at the time was also trying to hide the refugee process from the Dutch citizens. The truth was that most of the time the process for becoming a citizen totally random and not based on merit at all.

We also were learning that the Iranian consulate had back door dealings with the immigration office, and if they didn't like you for some reason it would be almost impossible to be approved. We were happy to try and get our story out to the public in hopes that it would move our case along, but in the end, we realized that the Iranian consulate was hearing our story too. They didn't look kindly on people that spoke badly about the government of Iran, and we suspected that they may have had a hand in our continuing denials. Whether that was true made no difference though in the end. Our situation was the same either way, and either way we had to find a way to stay in Holland.

There was a very nice woman named Helen that worked at the refugee office and would tell the church anything she heard about our case. One day she had told one of the church board members that our family was in danger, but that she didn't know why. There had been a lot of traffic in our home at that time with the press and members of the church always there sitting and talking with us. We had assumed it was because they had been excited by Amin's baptism and wanted to make sure that I too became Christian. However, once we heard this news that Helen had conveyed we realized that everyone had started coming to our house to support us and protect us.

A few days after the first alert came from Helen, Pastor Blenk and a few of the church board members came together to our house. It was then that they explained that they had found out that the immigration police were coming to take us for deportation on December the 4th. They told us this, but we didn't know what to think. I didn't even know that there was an immigration police, or that they had the authority to take us from our home without any notice. I could see by the looks on their faces though, that it was real and that this was a very serious situation.

Amin's niece Maryam who worked at a police station was also invited to come over that night. She arrived right in the middle of our conversations with the Pastor and the board members. She could see that I was terrified and in a complete state of worry. I sent the kids to their rooms to go to sleep and I could feel my stomach rumbling from anxiety and worry. After hours of talking about the situation we found out that once the immigration police have the deportation paperwork they can use it at any time they want to without any notice. Through their sources at the immigration office they could find out that our deportation paperwork had been sent to the immigration police already and that they could arrest us whenever they wanted, but that they had chosen December 4th as the date they would come. They had complete free reign to do anything to arrest us including to breaking down the door.

Maryam told us what she knew of the immigration police

as well, and it wasn't good news. She said that they are a department of the police force that was separate from the regular police. They were known for their cruelty and that they did not show any mercy for the families they were arresting. If you had too many denials, they had the right to arrest your entire family and take you to a horrible prison before finally sending you back to your home country. Maryam told us that when you enter the jail facility it's all made of all brick walls and that they hold you till the final verdict arrives and then blind fold you and take you to the airport. These details sent chills through my body, and the stress of the situation and begun to take its toll on Amin and me. We looked like we had been beaten up.

In the days that followed I tried to control my emotions around the kids, but eventually they could see past my short conversations and fake smiles. They could tell that there was something gravely wrong. They would ask me about what was going on, but I just kept telling them not to worry and that we were working with our friends at the church to make sure we would be able to stay in the Netherlands.

During this time, our church in Delft also began communicating with Farshid's church in Almere because they had experience in helping Iranian refugees with their cases. Farshid explained to our friends at the church in Delft that it was important that everything in their power was done to make sure we were not deported. He said that with all the press our story had received the Iranian consulate had surely taken notice, and that they were probably pushing the immigration office to expedite our deportation. He also explained that the authorities in Iran would also be sure to make an example of us if we were deported. The fact that Amin had converted to Christianity would be big news in Iran and it is considered the biggest sin of all. There was no way we'd be granted mercy by the Iranian authorities. He told Pastor Blenk that they must do something, anything, to prevent the immigration police from finding us. If that didn't happen and they did arrest us it would be too late, and our fate would be sealed.

The board members went into action immediately and enlisted the support of all their partner churches. They started a petition to keep us in the country and it was eventually signed by over 1500 Dutch families that all pledged their support to cause. They also gathered a list of people that offered to help support us financially as well as give us jobs and housing. They were hoping that with these pledges that the government would see that we would no longer be a burden on the government anymore, and let us stay. However, we soon learned that once the immigration police received those deportation papers it was difficult to stop the ball from rolling. Even the lawyers they had hired for us said that it was a long shot. They submitted the paperwork and told us to hope and pray for the best, but it was likely too late to do anything to save us. Our time was running out and they told us that all we could do was to wait a few weeks to hear back from the government.

This was a very dark time for Amin and me. We both cried a lot and felt completely helpless. Today when I look back at those days and try to share my experience on paper my heart aches and tears begin coming down my face because of all the hardships that we went through. While everyone was focused on how they could help us, I couldn't keep my mind off what would happen to us if we were deported. I would think to myself that we'd be killed for sure, but not in a normal way. They would torture us just to make an example to the rest of the county and to punish us for our sins. I had seen it numerous times on television and heard about how they tortured men physically and sexually abused the women before killing them.

The level of terror I was living with in my mind was overwhelming, and I finally decided that I would kill myself as well as my husband and our children before I'd let them send us back. I had convinced myself that a quick and painless death would be a great mercy to the people I cared about most in this world, compared to what we'd have to endure in Iran.

I tried to have less contact with my children after that. I would try and push them away from me by being mean to detach myself as much as possible from them. Amin tried to encourage me by telling me to have faith in God, and that we didn't know what could happen between now and December 4th.

"Why are you so angry?" He'd ask me, "Do you really want to make life for yourself and the kids hell until then? The kids are innocent in all of this. Why are you being are so mean to them?"

Of course, Amin didn't know what kind of thoughts that had been going through my head, and how I had planned to kill our entire family.

CHAPTER 14

I had a Dutch friend at the time named Ida. She was always full of love and acceptance toward me. Her love was like a mountain; unshakable. It seemed like no matter what I did or how I behaved she was there for me. She could see that I was slipping to the deepest depths of depression tried to do whatever she could to help me. She picked up the kids from school every day and would take them to her house so I would have one less thing to worry about. She could see that I had also not been so nice for the children to be around, and I'm sure she was doing it for their sakes as well. She told me that I was living my life like a prisoner on death row waiting to die. She had no idea of how correct she was with that statement.

Farshid's Iranian church began holding special prayer nights to pray for us to be spared from our deportation death sentence. It was a nice gesture, but I didn't care about God or any of it anymore. I was far away from everything in my mind. I would sit around and cry nonstop and chain smoke until I couldn't smoke anymore. I believed I was witnessing the last days of my life and I didn't want to talk to anyone or do anything. I wouldn't even pick up the phone to call my mother to see how she was doing with her cancer. It all started to fade away to me, and everything became meaningless. Time even seemed to move so slowly as if the clock wasn't moving at all, and the days and nights began to pass by so slowly.

The children were worried too, especially MJ who was old enough to understand that the situation was very serious. He tried to comfort his younger brother Omid, and at times he would even try to comfort Amin. He would talk about escaping into the woods so no one would be able to find us and that he'd help his dad build us a home out of wood. He had found this hope inside him somewhere and was excited to share it with us but I couldn't hear it. I could absorb any of it.

I complained constantly to God and asked him why he wasn't showing us mercy, "You are supposed to be a loving God! Why aren't you helping us? At least for our children. Why won't you spare their lives God? We aren't asking for too much. You created the whole universe, all we are asking for is your help to live a peaceful life."

I was grasping for anything, and was willing to pray to God even though I still didn't consider myself a full Christian. I was in an in between place with my religion. Not following Muslim traditions and not Christian either. Sometimes I thought maybe Allah was punishing us for considering Christianity.

Marian told me to read the Psalms of David, and that there were a lot of amazing and powerful prayers in it. At night while everyone was sleeping I would go into the kitchen and read it while streams of tears fell off my cheeks onto the kitchen table. I found some comfort while reading the Psalms of David. I thought it was good to know that I was not the only one that had gone through hardships, and that even David who had been favored by God had to go through hard times. I would burry myself in the word, but as soon as the sun would rise I found myself going back to that negative place and was full of sadness.

It was an unfamiliar place for me to be so deep in depression. It had seemed as though I could get through anything before in my earlier life in Iran. I had survived abuse from my brother, abuse from my husband, as well as horrible physical accidents with myself and my children, and yet back then I would always find a way to carry on. My family would always say, "Look at Sara, she always has hope and stays so positive no matter what." This time was different though. I had lost that inner light that I had before and had thrown in the towel on my life. It was late November of 1995, and December 4th was approaching fast. My options were slowly running out and I worried that I'd have to go through with my plan.

On Sunday morning of December first, the final countdown had begun in my head. Amin woke me up and told me to get ready to go to church. Unlike other Sundays when I would come up with 101 excuses as to why I couldn't go to church, this Sunday I jumped out of bed and scrambled to get ready very fast. I had a feeling that this was going to be the last time that I would see all the amazing people who loved and cared for us so much.

We got to church and were greeted by everyone with big hugs and encouraging smiles. They could see the despair on our faces. Pastor Blenk talked about our situation that day during the service and asked everyone to pray for us. They even scheduled a special nighttime service for us so everyone could come together one more time to pray for a miracle for us. Before that evening service began they wanted to have a private meeting with us at our home. Everyone was discussing all the possibilities for yet another time. I had found a little peace for some reason, almost as though I had come to terms with my fate and had accepted that the only humane thing to do was to kill myself and my family. Everyone noticed that I seemed to be in a lighter mood that night, but none of them could have imagined why.

During these conversations, someone brought up the idea that we should give up our kids for adoption so someone from the church or Amin's sister could adopt them and keep them safe. I couldn't believe what I was hearing. How was it possible that these people cared that much about my children? I hated myself because I saw how deep their love was for my children, and how I had given up and was going to destroy them.

I lost track of the conversation and was jolted back to reality when someone said that it had been decided and that on Monday they would go down to the social service office and find out what they had to do to adopt the kids. They asked Amin and I to please make sure to consider it and to make a final decision as soon as possible. After all the talking they prayed for us and they all left to go to the special service that the church was having. Amin and I didn't say a word to each other for hours after they left. Finally, after a while Amin decided to go to Bible study at one of the church members' house and left me alone in the house with the kids.

It was already dark by the time Amin left the house. I think the real reason he left was because he couldn't bear to see me so depressed like that. Ever since MJ's accident as a baby when we had made a shift in our marriage we began working as a team and always tried to fill our house with as much joy and laughter as possible. This new state of despair that I was dealing with was new for Amin and I'm sure he felt helpless to change it. Once I was alone I went to our room and sat by myself in the darkness. I began to cry out loud and beg God to spare us and just kept asking, "Why God, why?"

My cries must have very loud because the children came running into my room and hugged me asking if I was in pain from my hip injury. I told them that I was fine and not to worry. I sent them to their rooms and told them to go to sleep and be sure to shut the door. I didn't even want to hear them breathing with their doors open. I didn't want them to know the full depth of cruelty and injustice that this world is capable of. I wanted to close my eyes to it too. It is extremely hard for a mother to think about these things. I had planned in my head a 1000 times to end my own life as well as my children's and as much agony as this decision was causing me, I still knew it would be more humane than sending my family back to Iran. After I was sure the kids were sleeping, I went and cleaned the living room and took everything to the kitchen to wash so I could keep myself and my mind busy.

There was a heater in our kitchen that I would lean against whenever it was cold. That night was certainly chilly in our little apartment and after the dishes were finished I went over to the heater and leaned up against it to feel it's warmth. I began whispering to God with my usual thoughts when suddenly I saw a pale light outside the window. I figured it was our neighbors' son and his car who often came home drunk at night, but when I went over to investigate no one was there. The streets were quiet and dark without a single person roaming around. I was a little scared because I knew I had seen something and I just had a strange sense in the pit of my stomach.

I went back to the heater and turned back around to face the window. Sure, enough I could see the strange light again. I began wondering what on Earth it could be but before I could think too hard about it I noticed the light was moving and it was moving straight toward me.

Out of nowhere I heard a strong and calm voice say, "Have faith in me. Don't ever be afraid because I am here."

By that time, I felt as if the light had moved inside of body and was speaking directly to my soul, and as it faded away I became aware of my surroundings again and noticed that I was on my knees praying in the name of Jesus Christ in a way that I had never prayed before. It was much like how Farshid from Almere had prayed for us, and though I had been studying the Bible for some time at that point, I had never experienced anything like that. You never forget your first experience and your first touch from God in this way.

I don't know how long I was on my knees but after my prayer I felt physically lighter. There was a feeling of joy and gratitude in my heart that was so different from what I had felt just moments ago. Instead of complaining and yelling at God I was just saying thank you to him over and over in my head. and, a different joy and happiness was within me and I was constantly thanking God. The house was still completely dark. I had kept it extra dark on purpose because before this experience I wanted the room to match my mood of despair and depression, but after this I immediately walked around the whole house turned on all the lights. It was as if I wanted to spread this strange new joy I had in my heart to the rest of the house. I even went in and opened the kids' bedroom doors. All my previous plans of suicide and murder were completely gone. It was as if I had been miraculously renewed in my soul.

Right away I also called Pastor Blenk on the phone. He had just gotten home from the special prayer service that had been dedicated to us. He could immediately tell that my voice was shaking and that there was a sense of urgency in my tone. At first he was scared something bad had happened. I explained to him what had happened and I could hear him begin to laugh a loud grateful laugh. He started to thank God out loud, and told me that God had sent me a miracle by touching my heart and life in this way. I explained to him that even though none of our problems had disappeared in that moment, the miracle is that my heart is lighter and I am no longer crippled by fear. It doesn't even matter anymore to me if they send me to Iran or not. God spoke to me and told me to have faith in him and I had finally could hear Him.

I continued and told him that I only had one wish before I go back to Iran and that was to be baptized a Christian. This way if I am sent back at least I can go with a clean conscience. I want to go back with my heart and hands full of this love for Christ that I had found along our journey. I realized then that I had not been simply an immigrant to the Netherlands, but I was also an immigrant to Jesus Christ, and I wanted to bring back what I had found to share with others from my country. The Pastor was overjoyed with this news, and he assured me that I would be baptized before I was deported.

He said to them, "Do you bring in a lamp to put it under a bowl or a bed? Instead, don't you put it on its stand? - Mark 4:21

I began thinking about all the people at the church that night, and how they had been praying for us to be saved from the immigration police. However, prayers aren't always answered in the way you think they should be. God had not saved us from the immigration police yet, but he had already saved me from the darkness inside of me. He had a plan that was bigger than me or any of the other members of the church, and I could finally see that things happen per His timing. He can turn sadness and fear into joy and courage just from one touch, and that night I had witnessed the power of prayer. It's difficult to describe the incredibly light feeling I felt. I was brimming with happiness and couldn't help myself from skipping around the house. I went back to the kids' rooms and pulled them out of bed to hug them and kiss them. I couldn't stop loving them and thanking God for saving me before our story ended in tragedy. I knew then that the love of God is higher and more powerful than anything else, and that it had even influenced me to love my own children more intensely.

I could hardly wait for Amin to come home so I could share my happiness and joy with him. He had always stood my side for so many years through all our struggles. From the horrible pain, I went through with my hip, to all our issues in Iran, to our lives as refugees; he was there for me and I wanted him to be a part of this life-changing experience too.

Thankfully I had enough time freshen up before Amin got home because at that point I had been looking disheveled most of the time. I also set the table and made a nice meal for us to share once he returned. He opened the door shortly after I finished setting the dinner out and I ran up to him with a smile on my face and gave him a huge hug. I must have looked crazy because his immediate reaction was to ask if I was OK.

He said, "Has something happened? I know today is Sunday and the mail doesn't come on Sundays so it couldn't have been any good news in the mail. So, what in the world could have changed your attitude so drastically in the last few hours?"

I didn't know if I should smile or scream. I was so excited and overwhelmed with joy and I couldn't wait to tell him what had happened. Poor Amin was dizzy with confusion.

I began telling him everything that had happened in those few hours he was gone. I told him how while in the darkness of the house and being lost in hopelessness God sent me his light of forgiveness and love into my soul. He put me on my knees to pray and when I arose I felt the joy and happiness of the Lord inside my body and soul.

Amin smiled at me and simply said, "Thank God you are feeling better." He then got up and went to the bedroom without saying another word.

I was totally confused. He hadn't been swept away in my excitement and joy as I had hoped at all. It was as if he couldn't care less about this miraculous experience I had just had. I almost felt like he was jealous of my experience and somehow felt cheated by God. Our situation was the same as it had been a few hours earlier, and Amin was still feeling the despair and hopelessness that I had felt.

I waited for him to come back out so we could start our dinner but he was taking a very long time to return. I thought maybe he just wanted to go to bed early and wasn't interested in dinner. So, I went to the bedroom to talk to him. I wanted to tell him that everything was in God's hands and that we needed to have faith in Him. When I got to the bedroom I saw that Amin was on his knees between the two doors of his closet. He was praying but wasn't moving at all. He didn't even notice me at all and I left the room quietly. I left the room because I wanted to give him his privacy, but deep in my heart I knew something was happening to him too. God was going to touch him; it was no coincidence.

He finally came out of the bedroom a few minutes later. He seemed happier as well and with a shaking voice he started pray out loud thanking God. I asked him what had happened. He then told me, "You might not believe me, but I have been praying for a while and asking God to show himself to me or at least talk to me so my faith can grow more towards Him."

He continued, " When you told me about your encounter with God I was very happy for you but at the same time heartbroken. I complained to God that I have been asking you to show yourself to me or talk to me for a while but nothing. Yet you visited my wife today?

I listened without expression, and he continued his story.

"Then before I could even finish my thought, I heard a voice telling me **Get on your knees and have faith in me**. My knees went weak and my arms were locked into place, and without even trying I knelt and began to pray. While I was praying, I felt a warm feeling move through my body as if someone had put a warm hand on my shoulder. I just began thanking God over and over."

I realized that God had given Amin and me the same message that night. The message was to simply have faith in Him. That He is real and all we need to do is trust Him. I was so thankful for this amazing experience and that I could share it with Amin as we were facing such a difficult situation.

That night was beyond amazing for both of us and I can say that December 1, 1995 was the best and the most beautiful night of our lives. The next day the Pastor Blenk came over to our house to check-in on us and we told him all about Amin's experience too. I also reminded him that I needed to be baptized right away. I wanted to make sure that if I did have to go back to Iran and face my death, that I could bear all of it through my faith in God just as Christ had done.

The pastor's eyes were full of tears and he said, "In all my life serving God I have never seen a faith like you both have. Of course, all the Glory and honor goes to Him. I'm just overwhelmed by it all."

We only had a few days left until the immigration police were supposed to come and take us away, but in that short amount of time the mood in our house changed completely. The kids were happier and didn't worry about things because they saw that we weren't worried. We were full of the joy and love that God had restored in us, and that had put them at ease. We just focused on spending as much time together as a family as possible.

In fact, things changed so dramatically that MJ would ask me, "Mom, have they given us our citizenship? We aren't going to be sent back to Iran anymore?"

All I could tell him was that God was on our side and that no matter what happened we just needed to pray, and lean on God for support. There was nothing to be afraid of.

On that Tuesday, December 3rd., we received word that Helen from the immigration office confirmed to the church that we would were still scheduled to be arrested and deported on December 4th. She had told them that if they were going to do something drastic to save us it had to be done quickly. Technically the police could come even that night of the 3rd if they wanted to. Pastor Blenk asked everyone to pray for our safety that night so they would have time to figure out what they were going to do. The final countdown had truly begun, but I still was at peace. It was a true miracle to me no matter what happened to us physically.

The next morning was December 4th. The day had finally come. It had been quiet with no phone calls or visitors until around noon when one of the church board members arrived at our door. He came in and told us that we had to start packing because they were going to take us to a safe house so we could hide from the immigration police. I wasn't sure this was the best idea, and asked him, "How can I do that? I have two children in school. How can we just leave everything and hide out?"

He assured me that everything had been thought of, and

that they'd take care of it. He then repeated to us that we needed to start packing whatever we'd need to get by for a while, and that we'd leave first and the children would be brought to us in a few days. We'd also have to pack the entire apartment up so they could move our stuff into storage.

We had received so much love and generosity from these people that we trusted in them and their plan completely. So, Amin and I began packing. We had lived in that apartment for nearly two years by then and we had so much stuff that it was difficult to know where to start.

When the kids came home from school I explained the plan to them and I told them that we might have to be apart for a few days but that, God willing, everything would be ok very soon. Ida who was an incredible woman of God and always ready to serve, agreed to pick up the kids. The kids were a little concerned, but you could see that their trust in us as parents had also been restored and they agreed to stay with Ida.

The Iranian church from Almere was also in contact with us on a regular basis during those days, and when they found out that we were going to a safe house they immediately offered to come up and help get us ready. After I got off the phone with them I realized that I had given everything in the fridge to Ida to take it to her home for the kids. So, I didn't have much food left to feed a big group of people. Luckily they weren't planning on coming until eight o'clock that night so I thought that the small meal of chicken and rice I had made for Amin and I would be enough for people to snack on since they'd likely already have had dinner. Looking back on this now, it's funny to think about because hospitality is so important in the Iranian culture that even under these dire circumstances I was worried about taking care of our guests.

While we were packing, there was another knock on the door. I knew that it was too early for it to be our helpers from Almere and was curious to see who it was. I was hoping it wasn't the police.

I opened the door and found that it was an old friend from the refugee camp that was coming to see if he could stay for us for a night. Of course, with our commitment to hospitality, we invited him in. He immediately noticed that our house was torn apart and full of boxes and asked us if we were moving. We didn't want to make him feel bad for inconveniencing us so we didn't tell him anything about what was going on and just tried to change the subject. So, we sat and talked about his life and about what had happened at the refugee camp after we left. Then after an hour or so the doorbell rang and it was our friends from Almere. After they arrived our guest realized what was going on, and he pitched in along with everyone else to help get us packed.

I asked everyone if they had had dinner yet and they all told us that they had come straight from work and hadn't had a chance to eat. I told Amin to bring out everything that we had but that Amin and I wouldn't be able to eat. The grocery stores close at six o'clock so that was that. We didn't have enough but it was going to have to be good enough. Farshid noticed that I felt bad, and being Persian he understood how important it is to us to take care of our guests. He looked at me and said, "Dear sister, don't worry about it! We are going to do what Christ did when he prayed over the bread and the fish, and God blessed it. Thousands of people were fed when there had only been enough to feed a few. We are going to ask God to bless this meal as well."

I had seen the Life of Christ movie a few times by then and every time I saw that scene tears would roll down my face. It is such a moving story. So, I decided to let it go and know that God was blessing our meal no matter how big it was. Farshid prayed over the meal, and soon another group of people from the church showed up to help us. Farshid invited them all in and told them to take plates and help themselves. Our house was packed with helpers! Somehow they all were fed and happy. We truly saw it as another miracle from God. A meal for two people had fed over eight adults and were even leftovers after they were done.

And Jesus saith unto them, How many loaves have ye? And they said, Seven, and a few little fishes. And he commanded the multitude to sit down on the ground.And he took the seven loaves and the fishes, and gave thanks, and brake them, and gave to his disciples, and the disciples to the multitude.

- Matthew 15:34-36

After Dinner, we all started packing again. Everyone oversaw a section and even our guest from the camp helped. Our friends had rented a huge truck and within hours they had packed it with everything from our house. They also took Amin's car to the storage unit outside of town where all our other things were to be stored. When everything was done, we got in the car to go to our new home that had been arranged for us. We felt bad leaving our friend from the refugee camp so one of our friends from the church in Delft offered to take him in for the night. Nobody was to know where our new home was going to be. Only a couple of the church board members knew where it was.

During the final discussions, it was decided that Amin not come with me to the safe house right away, and that it would be better if he went to Almere for a little while. It would be more difficult to track us if we weren't together and it would be good for Amin to spend some time in the church there. Farshid assured me that there were always a lot of people at his house in Almere and that Amin would never feel lonely or uncomfortable. So, we agreed to this new plan.

We hugged each other and said our goodbyes then went our separate ways. It was impossible to not feel emotional. Not having Amin there was like a piece of me was missing, and the kids were with Ida. I felt very alone, but hopeful that we'd all be reunited soon.

Cor drove me to a home I did not know just inside the city center of Delft. It was owned by a nice woman from the church named, Mrs. Fiet. As soon as I came into her home I noticed how nicely decorated and organized everything was. She had been praying all night on her knees for our safety, and was so glad I had arrived safely to her. She gave me a huge hug and I immediately felt at ease with her. She guided me upstairs to her attic to the room they had prepared for us. When I walked in I realized that this was no ordinary attic, but that she had taken a lot of time to make sure it was perfect for us. It was more like an attic suite then anything. Mrs. Fiet said that she had always kept her attic this way so it would be ready to be used for the good of God's kingdom and His children.

There was a special place for MJ and Omid to sleep in, as well as a place for Amin and me to rest and sleep that was a little separated. To my shock, it also had a small kitchen. Mrs. Fiet asked me if I was afraid, and told me that if I was she would stay with me. I thanked her and told her that I was fine. She was such a thoughtful and kind woman with the warmest heart. She smiled and left me alone to get settled. When I was alone I felt very awkward and began thinking to myself about all the dramatic changes that had happened in our lives in just a few short hours. My husband was in Almere, my kids weren't with me either, and I began to see myself as being all alone. However, after the miracle I had witnessed of God's love I still had a sense of hope, and that comforted me. It was going to be a completely different way of life. Almost like a secret life. It had shaken me up quite a bit.

My mind wandered throughout the night and I was thinking that God must be testing us or preparing us to be apart from each other, or perhaps it was just the beginning of our new path. The possible outcomes to our future kept rolling around in my head repeatedly. I walked around smoking until the sun rose the next morning, but unlike usual, I wasn't crying uncontrollably from the burden of our problems. The crying had been a sign of hopelessness, and though I was worried, God had filled me with hope and faith in His plan. I prayed and asked God to give me peace so I would be able to go through all these problems successfully. I spent that entire morning just being present with God and praying.

The next day Pastor Blenk was the first person to contact me. He wanted to know how I was doing and when he heard the tone of my voice his mood lightened a bit. He could tell that I was still leaning on God for support. He told me not to worry about a thing and that I would only have to be separated from the kids for 48 hours so they could monitor what the police were doing. He told me that he would keep me updated always. I asked him how long we'd have to stay away from our home, and he answered, "If God's hand is on your life you don't have to worry about it. God will use all of us to keep you guys safe and to give you peace."

His words pierced my heart and gave me so much hope and strength even though I was alone. At times, I still looked back over all the experiences we had since we had come to the Netherlands, but now I had a different perspective on things. I thanked God because he had put us in all those situations so we could believe in his son Jesus Christ.

The night we left our home had caused quite a stir with the neighbors. People were wondering why we were moving in the middle of the night. One of our neighbors that was very caring and concerned about our situation came out to ask if we were OK. One of the people from the church had told her a fake explanation, but also asked her if she wouldn't mind keeping an eye on our home while we were away. She agreed to help and told him that she'd watch the house for us. It was a good plan. This way we'd be able to see if the police were planning on raiding our house.

Then Jesus asked them, "Would anyone light a lamp and then put it under a basket or under a bed? Of course not! A lamp is placed on a stand, where its light will shine.

Mark 4:21

CHAPTER 15

The next day I started to study the word of God when Mrs. Fiet came upstairs and brought me lunch. After lunch she asked me to go downstairs and talk with her. Initially I was a little worried and asked her if anything had happened. She explained that everything was fine, and that there were a couple people from church that wanted to come see me. Mrs. Fiet could see that I was a little hesitant and wasn't sure I was ready to accept visitors yet. She said, "I want you to remember that you are a very strong and faithful woman of God, and He is going to help you no matter what. There is always tests and temptations in a life of a believer, but also remember that God always takes care of his children."

She began talking about her own life and how God has blessed them so much, and how wealthy they had been. She told me how they had a major share in Shell Oil in England and the Netherlands at one time. They were successful beyond their dreams until they had lost much of their wealth and almost became bankrupt. God protected them and made sure there were provided for even in the worst situation. She was saying that in everyone's life's there are obstacles and tests.

It reminded me of the story in the Bible when Satan was given permission from God to tempt or confuse Job. He took his wealth, his children and so much more but Job never lost his faith in God and he proved to Satan that God's children will always have in him no matter what. Job's faith was greatly tested but when he proved his faith in God, God blessed him even more than before. Job's life is a testament. Satan had told God that if God took all of Job's wealth and his children, Job would lose his faith and turn his back on God. "Oh you think Job is faithful, he won't be if you take all of his blessings away."

Mrs. Fiet said, "This has happened in our lives as well but

God wanted to save us and today because of his love and mercy we still have this house and we want to use it for his glory and for people who are going through tough times."

She told me not to ever feel like a guest at the house because it was God's Home and they are just God's servants. When she was talking about all these things I was thinking to myself, "Wow God has given her and her husband such huge spirits to want to serve God so freely. I had not yet seen her husband, but I knew he must be a wonderful man to open his house like this to us. I asked her where he was and she explained that he wanted to give me some space before introducing himself. He worked from home and didn't want to make me feel uncomfortable. Mrs. Fiet said that he sends his greetings and is praying for your family so that you may overcome this test.

While we were talking two of the leaders of the church showed up and they told us that the immigration police had gone to our house in the early morning hours, and when they didn't see us there they had placed a few officers there so they can monitor our house. They even asked some of the neighbors about us, but nobody gave them any information. Everyone from the church was so grateful for our safety, but also shaken up. Before we came along they had relatively quiet lives with little threat of danger. They had never known someone or been so close to a difficult refugee situation like ours. Some were afraid that they could get in trouble for passing on the secret information from the immigration police. In truth, they could have been in serious trouble if it was ever proven. It was an amazing expression of love and generosity that they went through these hardships for us. Our level of thankfulness could not be fully expressed with just words.

After the first 48 hours in Mrs. Fiet's attic, the kids finally came over. I realized how much I had missed them and at the same time I missed Amin. I was talking to Amin every day so we would support each other but it was still very difficult to be apart. My job at that time was to stay by the window and watch people who were walking in the area, or study the bible and pray, or pace back and forth all day while I waited for the kids. That's how I would spend my days while the kids were at school. When they would get home they would ask for their father repeatedly. It was becoming hard for us to be separated from Amin so we asked the elders of the church if they could arrange a trip to Almere so the children could see their father. They agreed and that Friday night a car came to take us to be with Amin.

The kids were full of happiness and joy when they saw their dad. It also seemed like Amin was having a good experience with Farshid's family who had amazing and loving parents. Farshid's mother was a very nice and loving lady who they called Mama Farah. Her husband was called Papa Jamal. He was a very quiet and humble person and I could tell that Amin liked him very much. Farshid also had 3 other siblings and his fiancée, and sister. Amin seemed very comfortable and relaxed with them. I was surprised because he was usually so shy. Though this was not your typical Persian family, and so very different than what we had gone through with our own. They were so full of love and positivity. They also knew that Amin was very new into Christianity and wanted him to feel like he could come to them with questions. It was obvious that they had all formed a very strong bond.

Being around Christians that were also Persian had a very deep effect on Amin, and I could tell right away that he had also grown in his faith for God. That night they had decided to have a special dinner to give thanks a praise to God in honor of our family being reunited. They made a delicious meal for us, and we all shared our stories of the past few weeks. They were so amazing and loving, it truly seemed like they were family.

It was late that night when I was alone with Mama Farah when she told me that she wanted me to think of this home as my own. She told me that she knew me a little bit through Marjan, and we know that your home was always open to everyone, and now we have opened our home for you. "I was shocked that the last night you were there you still were trying to take care of all your guests! Even the one that showed up without notice, you took him in! Just remember that we have been praying for your salvation for months, and we consider you part of our family."

Her words gave me so much hope and she told me that God test his children who he loves the most, so we can grow to be stronger and shine in his glory. She talked about many of the prophets in the Bible. She said, even though they were called by God they had been put through tests and always stayed strong in their faith. She was more than just a friend. She had a wonderful maternal quality to her spirit and that was very comforting to me.

We stayed there for the entire weekend and the kids didn't want to leave without their father. First we prayed about it and after that we discussed it with the leaders of the Dutch church and they concluded that Amin should come back with us if he stayed at home and did not go outside at all. So, we left to go back to Delft and stay in Mrs. Fiet's attic, but this time as a complete family. We were still worried about our situation, but nothing was more comforting than having us all back safely under the same roof.

When we got back to the attic, I began to realize how much Amin had grown spiritually while he was in Almere. He was filled with so much hope and humbleness, and his speech was different than before. I would look at him and see a different man who was filled peace in his spirit. His hair was starting to turn slightly white and I didn't know if it was from gaining more wisdom or from the pressure of life in those days but whatever it was from, he was changing. It had given me a lot of strength and courage to continue my journey in learning the Bible as well. I was very happy that he had come back to us so we could study the word of God together, and of course also to divide some of the responsibilities of the house.

I became very nostalgic during this time and began to look

back on how our life had changed so much over the past few years. We left Iran and immigrated to the Netherlands with so much hope in our hearts, and even if or living conditions were small we always had room for someone in need. I saw that now another door had opened for us in the tiny attic, and though they didn't have much, the Fiets made sure there was room for us. This attic was a sanctuary. A house full of peace and the love of God but we still didn't know if we'd be caught and sent back to our deaths in Iran. We had come to realize that all we had was our salvation in Jesus Christ, and to our surprise, that was all we needed.

At times, I would thank God that he didn't give our citizenship in the Netherlands so we could go through the hardships that brought us to be saved by Jesus Christ. I also thanked him for allowing us to build a personal and direct relationship with him even though we didn't deserve it. Beyond the fact that we had lied about Amin's baptism, we had been taught in Islam that we could not have a personal relationship with God at all.

In Islam, we had to pray to the 12 prophets of Islam because they had a direct relationship with Allah and through our sacrifices and prayers to them, we could ask Allah for things. There is a book named "The Visit of Ashoora" and another book called "Souraye Tavasool" that are both meant to be studied strictly to become closer to Allah. The problem was that these books are written in Arabic and we don't understand Arabic. A westerner unfamiliar with these traditions may wonder how we could even understand what we were saying in our prayers. The truth was that nobody else would know if it was right or wrong either. The answer was always that Allah would know and only understand your prayers if they were in Arabic.

I found many examples in my previous religion that seemed odd to me now, and I wondered how I had ever believed them to be true. For instance, there is a holy city in Iran called

"Ghom". People go to the city specifically to pray for healing, and several thousand travel there each year. It is considered holy because the daughter of one of the prophets was buried there and they had made her grave a shrine. Her grave has a gold metal cage surrounding it and it's very ornate. People looking for help from Allah travel there and cry, pray, and then throw money into the golden cage on top of the holy grave so the girl can bring their prayers to her brother, and her brother can then bring those prayers to Allah. All of these strange rituals just to talk to Allah. I loved that now in Christ I could talk to my Father God directly and feel his love for me.

Another example in the Islamic religion that I kept thinking about was a place called "Jamkaran" just outside of the city of Ghom. It is in this place where they say the last prophet emerged out of a pit. People traveled all over to pray a special prayer at Jamkaran called the "Emam Zaman" or "Mahdi" while they threw money down the pit with their letters of requests. I don't know why I never asked myself why there would be a prophet coming out of a pit, but it seemed almost absurd to me now. I think it was because I had been living in the dark and never knew any better. I had not experienced any light in my heart so I could not yet compare the darkness to the light until I became a follower of Jesus Christ.

Things had changed by then though, and I could clearly see the light from the dark. I trusted God to lead me down the right path, the path that He had chosen for us. It was an exciting time for Amin and I when we could devote practically all our time to learning God's word in the Bible. It was as if the attic was our university and the Holy Spirit was our teacher, always leading us to ask questions about what we were learning. Sometimes I would just read aloud to Amin for hours from the Bible and we both just soaked it all up. We weren't able to go anywhere in the first weeks so we just continued to stay in the attic studying. It might sound boring to others, but to us it was an awakening. We got to spend so much time with Jesus and the Word of God, and it filled our hearts to the brim with love.

One night after we had all gone to sleep, I had a dream where someone with a loud voice told me that I would be back to my own house within 29-40 days. The voice told me not to worry about anything because we will be taken care of. When I opened my eyes, I started to give thanks to God because of this new hope and peace he had given me from this dream. I started to feel safe and warm, and quickly fell back to sleep.

The next morning when Ida came to pick up the kids she could see that I was in a very happy mood, and asked me what was going on. I immediately told her about my dream from the night before, but to my surprise she wasn't as excited about it as I was. She had a concerned look on her face and then told me that she had read in a book that Middle Eastern people dream a lot, and they are very emotional and believe everything they think they feel. My mood was a little deflated and I after thinking for a second I wondered if maybe she was right. I did dream a lot and I did analyze every emotion. I was making too much of it. I tried to brush it off and move on. I was supposed to go with Ida to her house for a special baking day that day with some of the ladies from church and didn't want to spoil it.

So, we all went to Ida's home with her. She took the kids to school and then came back to get the baking supplies ready. We started to bake and of course talking while we baked. We had an amazing time together. She treated me like I was the head of the house and let me make all the decision while we baked. That afternoon some of the ladies from church came over as well to see me. They were so loving and they offered to help me if there was anything we needed. They even offered to go to the Dutch government on our behalf. We all spent the day catching up and they even told me about some news I wasn't aware of. Apparently, there were some articles written about us after we had left our house that were very harsh concerning their opinion of the Dutch government. They didn't understand why they would treat a family like ours this way, especially with the support of the church. There were even interviews with families from all over Holland that were supporting our cause.

I was truly thanking God that he had placed us in a country that was so full of love and that through these hardships we had never walked alone, and always had these people supporting us. As the day went on the ladies started asking me about how things were going, and I started telling them about how wonderful it had been so far. I also started talking about our future and the kids' future. I soon noticed that many of the ladies were whispering to each other about how calm I seemed. I knew it was the peace in my heart that because of my faith in God.

Shortly after we had coffee and cakes it was time for me to go back to the Fiets' house. When I got back to the attic I was so excited to tell Amin about everything that had happened that day, but right away I could see that he wasn't in the mood for it. I asked him what was wrong, and he told me that he had just been extremely bored when I was gone and that he had realized that he missed working very much. Amin was a very hard workingman and he had worked since he was a teenager. Now that he was stuck in an attic and couldn't do anything at all, he was going crazy. So, we decided after the kids went to sleep that night that we would go downstairs and talk to Mrs. Fiet and maybe we could figure out a way to help Amin work without leaving the house. Mrs. Fiet was always excited to talk with us and so she asked us to sit down. First she asked about my day with Ida and I had brought her a piece of cake that we had baked that day. I explained our reason for our talk and then asked if she had any remodeling that needed to be done or if there was anything in the house that needed to be fixed. She thought it was a great idea for Amin to help with projects around the house. She said that someone like Amin needs to keep his hands busy, and that she'd talk it over with her husband and see what they could do.

After she had spoken to her husband, she then asked Amin

to come back downstairs. She immediately told him that they had decided to remodel their entire bathroom! It was such a blessing to Amin because right after that he would begin working on the project. Mrs. Fiet's husband would go buy the tools and the supplies and Amin began to demolish the bathroom so they could then build the new one.

After our meeting, we went back upstairs and just like every night I would read from the Bible and then we'd go to sleep. Again, this night I had an odd dream. A loud voice then woke me up. It was just like the voice from the night before that was in my dream. It told me "Didn't I tell you not to worry and that you will be going back to your house within 29-40 days? Why do you doubt me?"

I started to cry and ask for forgiveness. I told God that I was just a baby believer, new in my faith. I begged him to help me and that I would promise never to doubt Him ever again." While I was crying, and begging God to help me, Amin woke up and asked me what had happened. I immediately told Amin about my dreams, but he did know what to make of it.

The next day I decided not to share or talk to anyone about either of my dreams. I knew that God would take care of things on His time, and until then I would not waste a minute. I would spend all my time instead, buried in the Word working toward my baptism. I had decided that I would be baptized at any price and I couldn't wait to finally officially become a Christian. Because I knew there was no way to be baptized in Iran, I became obsessed with making sure it was done as soon as possible. This way if we were deported we could face any hardship or threat upon our lives with our heads lifted high knowing that we had been forgiven through the blood of Christ. I kept asking our pastor repeatedly, "When can I be baptized? How long will it be before I can be baptized?"

Pastor Blenk was very loving and supportive and encouraging me to wait until the proper time. One day he said to me, "I am sure that you believe in Christ and have the love of God in your heart, but what do you know of the Word? The church requires that you complete the proper schedule of classes before you can be baptized."

I looked at him and asked, "Where in the Bible does it say that you need classes to become a believer and follower of Jesus Christ? I have accepted Jesus into my heart, and now I am ready to be baptized in his name."

And as they went on their way, they came unto a certain water: and the eunuch said, See, here is water; what doth hinder me to be baptized? And Philip said, If thou believest with all thine heart, thou mayest. And he answered and said, I believe that Jesus Christ is the Son of God. – Acts 8:36-37

I continued to tell him about how my intense study, "I read the Word of God for hours every night, and yes it's true that we don't have an official teacher, but we've asked God to send the Holy Spirit to be our teacher. We've prayed that God would open our understanding of the Word as we study it. Please, you know our situation and I cannot be sent back to Iran without this blessing and honor. I beg you to talk to the board members to see if they might make an exception. I believe in Christ with all of my heart, and I am ready."

The pastor was moved by these words and he could see that I wanted this more than anything in the entire world. He looked at me as his eyes began to tear up and said, "My daughter don't worry. You are going to be baptized very soon. I am going to have and meeting with the board members right away to get their approval, and will let you know what date you will get baptized."

This was a huge breakthrough for me, and for the church itself. This church was very traditional, and never had they, in all its history made an exception like this. I was beyond grateful for Pastor Blenk's empathy and support in this. I had found this amazing, life-changing relationship with God and Christ, and wanted to shout it from the rooftops. This was the first time I had ever had something like this in my life. It was so precious to me because it had not been forced upon me by my parents, but something I had struggled on my own to find. Islam was my heritage, but this path was chosen for me by God and nobody could ever take it away.

SECTION 5

CHAPTERS 16 - 21

The remaining chapters of the book follow Sara and her family through their journey in discovering the Word of God, the birth of a new child, and many more hardships and obstacles in their immigration case.

They are taken by the church into hiding so that they will not be arrested and deported, and eventually back to their own home. Through it all the Dutch media covered the details of their story, and appealed to the Dutch people for help. At one point they even had a petition with over 2,000 signatures sent on their behalf to protest their immigration status.

There are also many incredible stories of how they helped others in need over the 7 long years they were in The Netherlands, even though they themselves never had a secure position for their family. Always reaching out to others both in the Dutch community and in the Iranian community to share their conversion experience.

Many people helped them along the way and sacrificed to try and keep them safe and in The Netherlands. However, in the end the Lord had other plans for them, and after starting the first Iranian outreach church services ever in the city of Delft, they were given asylum in the United States. This is still where they live to this day and continue to do God's work.

CHAPTER 16

Staying at Mrs. Fiet's home was such a blessing. We read and studied the Bible together in her kitchen each day, and each day I would ask her question after question about the Word. She had a tremendous level of faith, and always answered my questions in humbleness and love. She was the one that taught me pray each time I read the Bible, and to ask God to open His Word for me through the Holy Spirit. I could feel myself growing closer to God each day. While it was not ideal that we had to live in someone's attic, I look back and think it was all part of God's plan for us. Because we were required to stay inside almost all the time it left me with a lot of free time and just Like Amin, I needed to find work to keep myself busy. In my case, I found that my work was studying the Word of God. Whenever the children were at school or were sleeping, I was working.

I felt renewed through my passion for learning about the Bible, but there was still one issue that began to bother me, and that was my smoking. My smoking had always bothered my husband, but I never felt the urge to quite to appease him. Since I had started on my journey to becoming a Christian however, this self-destructive habit began to tug at my conscience. It just didn't feel quite right, then one afternoon I came across the following passage, "Don't you know that you yourselves are God's temple and that God's Spirit dwells in your midst? If anyone destroys God's temple, God will destroy that person; for God's temple is sacred, and you together are that temple," Corinthians 3:16-17.

I realized as I read it that this passage was directly speaking to me about my smoking. I immediately got up from my study and ran to grab my pack of cigarettes. I pulled one out and before I lit it I said, "OK God, you know how much I love smoking, and I have put up with Amin's complaining for years just so I could enjoy my cigarettes. Today though I want to quit God... because you said in your Word that our bodies are temples where you dwell, and that they are sacred. So, that's it Lord. I ask you to help me stop smoking so I can do no further harm to your temple. I ask you to help me make sure this is my last cigarette."

I then lit what would be my last cigarette and I smoked it furiously, puffing away until it was gone. I then threw it on the ground and stomped on it with the conviction to never do it again to honor God. God's miracles come in all shapes and sizes, and I know that God helped me quit smoking that day. After that moment I could set smoking aside completely, and truly never had another urge to smoke again. This made me realize that God loves us on all levels, and wants to help us change the root of all negativity in our lives. No matter what happened with our immigration case I felt like God had already touched our lives in so many ways, and I was so grateful for this.

In the meantime, we still had no idea what was going on with our immigration case. We had averted arrest, but for how long? Helen from the immigration office was still talking to the church board members on a regular basis, and though she didn't have any news about a change in our deportation order, she did tell them that the immigration officers had been dumbfounded by our late-night escape and spent a lot of time investigating the case. They had interviewed all our neighbors in an attempt to find out where we had gone. We were updated on any news quite often, but I think they deliberately left us out of the loop sometimes just to keep us from worrying. Instead, they helped us focus on the positives in our lives which most often centered around church and my upcoming baptism.

A few weeks after my baptism talk with Pastor Blenk we received the good news that the church board members had agreed, and they had scheduled my baptism as well as the children to take place on December 24th. I was overjoyed at this news and couldn't wait for Christmas to arrive. We also learned that the church had requested for us to come and answer a few questions about our faith at the Pastor's home before the baptism could take place. I knew just how traditional this church was, and I also knew that they didn't ever bend their rules on anything, for anyone. So of course, I agreed to go to the interview at Pastor Blenk's house to discuss my faith and why I felt I should be baptized. I was honored that they were willing to accept us with open arms and hearts, and that they even considered making an exception to their rules for us. This would be the first time that the church would baptize someone who had not gone through the long list of classes that were normally required.

The night of the interview came and we all went over to Pastor Blenk's home. Even if I should have been, I was not nervous at all. I knew that my faith was real, and that this would shine through. I can say now looking back that this interview night was one of the most blessed and moving evenings I had ever had. We answered questions about our faith with the genuine excitement we had in our hearts for studying the Word of God. We talked for quite some time about our knowledge of the Bible and they could see that we had been taking our personal studies seriously. After these formalities, we were then given the opportunity to give our testimony and to speak about how God had touched our lives so many times as we were going through the hardships with our immigration status. After this conversation, we could see that it was much easier for the board members to make their final decision. They told us that we were a testimony for them as well. They had seen God work miracles in our lives too, and it had strengthened their faith at the very same time. They trusted our word, and they assured us that the baptism would take place on Christmas, December 25 as planned.

Everything seemed to be working out per God's plan, and I was so thankful that my biggest dream of all was going to come true: to be baptized as a Christian. It was during this time however that we learned some devastating news concerning Amin's brother who had helped us so much when we had first come to the Netherlands. We found out that Amin's niece, the daughter of his brother, worked at the immigration police department that was handling our case. She had our deportation paperwork in her hands and decided to alert us of the situation. We knew that her father had to have told her to not reach out to us, and this sentiment was solely based on the conflict that we had had with his wife.

I thank God that he used other people to help us like Helen. She wasn't our blood relative, and she hadn't even known us personally beforehand. Yet God moved something in her spirit to help us so we could escape before our arrest. This experience showed us that we should never lean on a man, but to rather lean on God. Everything is under His control and all we need to do is to stay faithful. We prayed for Amin's brother and their family to soften their hearts toward us so they could be healed from the destructive hate they had in their hearts. This was heart-wrenching for Amin, and if we had not had the support of our church family I don't think he would have could deal with it. He had lost one brother but instead God had given him hundreds of other brothers in Christ.

Finally, after what seemed like an eternity, the day of my baptism arrived. It was a cold Sunday around Christmas time. It was so cold that you could see your breath while sitting inside the Old Church. This beautiful historic church was built entirely out of stones and brick, and felt like a freezer. There were even special places under the pews for people to bring a personal heater. I didn't let the cold bother me though. Today was going to be a turing point in my life, and that was all I was focused on. Many people came from all over Holland that day to support us. Even a few from Krimpen! They had heard through the grapevine of my baptism and came to show their support.

Finally, after everyone was settled Pastor Blan began to speak, "It is an honor to for our church to baptize this incredible Muslim family that we have all gotten to know and love."

I couldn't stop the tears from rolling down my face. My heart was aching just thinking about what we had done when Amin was baptized by tricking the church and being arrogant enough to try and trick God. I was so grateful for this opportunity to not only be baptized, but also to make things right between the church and our family. The pastor continued his message and started talking about Ruth. Right then I began to daydream about Christ, and how when he was upon the cross he had asked God to "Forgive them Father, for they know not what they do," Luke 23:34.

I asked God to forgive me right then, for the countless time, and in that moment, I was simply overjoyed that I had come to know the one and only true God. God who loves us unconditionally and always gives us opportunities for forgiveness. With my baptism that day my old self would die. I would bury my old self and my sins and begin a new life fully living in Christ. The service was amazing and so full of warmth and love that the cold was barely noticeable any more. Then at the end I was baptized by our beloved Pastor Blenk.

After the service, we were standing for about an hour because there was a huge line of people who wanted to shake our hands in congratulations and give us huge hugs. I had truly found a new family in Christ that cared for us like nobody ever had before. At the same time the members of the church would say that we were a gift from God for them as well. From either perspective, God's work is amazing, and our shared experience was a testament to God's love.

Tiny and Cor left quickly after the service to prepare for the celebration that was to be at their house after church. We followed shortly after, and were absolutely amazed at the outpouring of support from everyone. People came to Cor and Tiny's house nonstop throughout the day until sunset! Everyone came to give their good wishes and to spend time fellowshipping with our church family, and of course to share in coffee and cakes as well. By the end of it all I was exhausted, and my pain from my accident with a truck in Iran was starting to flare up. I asked Cor if he could take us home, and we all piled into his car to head back to our attic suite at Mrs. Fiet's house.

That day was one of the most beautiful and unforgettable days of my life. Even today when the pastor does an alter call and asks the members of the church to go up to help pray for people, I think back to the beginning days of my salvation and how awesome and exciting it was being a follower of Jesus. I love praying to God to touch me once again like before just so I could experience that same level of excitement that I had in the beginning. We always must ask God to help us be refreshed in our faith and keep the passion in our hearts for Christ and God's love.

I was living a life full of darkness with a burden on my shoulders and after that day I felt those chains being broken of my life with God's help. Now I was feeling like a new person in Christ. Up until yesterday I was living a life full of sin and blinded by the negativity of life but today I want to live my life in the light of God; for God. I used to be afraid of not knowing what tomorrow might hold for us, but today I know that God knows everything. he knows what is going to happen tomorrow and the next year. He even has counted the hairs on my head! There was nothing left to fear because God has it. I put my complete faith in Him. That night I went to sleep calmly without anxiety, trusting in the Lord.

It was exactly one week after my baptism, and it was exactly 29 days since I had that dream where God told me we'd be returning to our home within 40 days. Nothing had happened in regards to our case yet, but I kept praying to God that the dream was right and that we'd have a breakthrough and can return to our home. Amin had been working very hard over the previous few weeks and had finished the remodel of the bathroom. Mrs. Fiet and her husband were ecstatic and insisted on paying Amin for the job. How could we accept anything from these amazing people who had opened their home and heart to us in our incredible time of need? Amin explained that the pleasure had been his, and that if they were happy with the results that were all the payment he needed. It was as if were one big happy family living there with them. We continued to spend hours studying the Bible together and going about life as usual. They were such a blessing.

For MJ and Omid though they longed to get back to our old house and to their own rooms. Most nights they would ask us when we'd be able to go back, and how long would it be before they could see their friends outside of school. They were like prisoners once they left school. Even during the school day was stressful for them. All their friends and teachers were on high alert in case an immigration officer came asking questions about them. Some nights Omid would also have nightmares. He would wake up screaming and crying, and sometimes his nose would be bleeding. We weren't sure why this was happening, but both children's health suffered during this time, and we believed that it was directly related to the amount of pressure and stress that they had to endure.

Omid's nosebleeds became more frequent and his nose would bleed so badly that it became difficult to stop the bleeding. Cor was concerned about Omid and reached out to one of the doctors in the church who told him that it could be a very dangerous situation and that we'd have to have the blood vessels in his nose frozen. My residual pain from my accident was getting very bad at that time too, but with everything going on it was all I could do just to focus on Omid and comfort him. Mrs. Fiet was a huge help at night as well, and would tell the children to pray to God for healing. She also tried to reassure them by saying that God had taken care of us so far and that he would continue to watch over us. We also tried not to mention any bad news around the kids and shield them from the reality of the situation.

It was during this time as well that MJ began to have

massive headaches throughout the day. Even during school, he suffered and had to spend a lot of time in the nurse's office instead of learning. We were of course immediately concerned about this because of MJ's brain hemorrhage that he had when he was a baby. He had been completely normal after that, and had luckily not suffered from seizures like the doctors had predicted. However, with our current situation, Amin and I worried that all the stress was going to trigger something to do with MJ's prior injury. I would ask God to put us through any kind of test that He wanted, but to please spare the kids. Their pain is the one thing that I couldn't bear. We were getting closer to the end of winter and spring was just around the corner. I prayed to God constantly to change our situation because of the kids' health or to find a way to help them be healthy and stress free.

40 days had passed since my dream and on the 40th day I waited all day for a news. I was praying the whole time asking God, "OK Lord, the 40th day is here and I beg you to show me a sign. I need to know what is going to happen on this day that you have shown me in my dream."

Amin had gone that day to the storage facility they had for us outside of town to help someone out, and to bring over a few of our things. Time was going by very slow, and by two o'clock in the afternoon, nothing had happened. I was on my knees praying and begging God when suddenly I started to sob and even cry out, and just let all the emotions I'd been holding onto out. I cried so much that I lost track of time and didn't even notice when the kids got home. Mrs. Fiet had let them in and when they came up the stairs they heard my crying. They didn't want to disturb me, so without a word they both crept down the stairs where they sat together and cried too. After a few moments, they went downstairs and told Mrs. Fiet that there was something wrong with their mother because she is crying upstairs uncontrollably. She gave them a snack and calmed them down a bit, then went upstairs to check on me.

I was lost in my prayers and emotional release when I felt a warm hand on my shoulder, then Mrs. Fiet began calling my name. She asked me, "Sweetheart, what's wrong? Why are you so sad, and why are you crying?"

Before I could answer her question, I realized that the kids should've been home by then. I jumped up and asking, "Where are the kids? Are they OK?"

Mrs. Fiet tried to calm me down and told me not to worry about the kids because they were downstairs with her husband. "When they came home and came upstairs they saw that you were crying, and asked me to come up to pray with you."

Even as she talked to me I couldn't stop crying. Now that I am writing this down years later, there are tears in my eyes and the scars of that day have become new again. It was a breaking point, and I was unloading all my pent-up frustrations. When she saw that I wouldn't stop crying she called Cor and told him that she didn't know what was wrong with me, but that I was inconsolable and hadn't stopped crying for hours. Cor came over and he and Mrs. Fiet tried their best to comfort me, "You can't be worried like this now," they said. "God has been with you all so far and has protected you. You have to stay strong and trust that he has a plan for you."

Eventually I did calm down a little and became very embarrassed as I realized how many people were worried about me. I asked them to forgive my foolishness, and they both smiled and hugged me. The children came upstairs after that and hugged me too. MJ said, "Mom, have Aunty Fiet pray for you because we were crying as well and when she prayed for us we felt much better."

I was embarrassed that the kids had to see me like that. I was even a little jealous of their innocent faith. Mrs. Fiet then told us to all hold hands and to pray together because God loves to hear all our voices. Omid started to pray with his childlike voice and asked God to help Mom stop crying, and for us to go back home so he could get his room back. He looked at me and smiled after he was done, and I could feel my strength coming back just by looking at his face.

After Omid, MJ then also started to pray. Listening to his prayers, Mrs. Fiet started to cry. It was such a sweet, young prayer. It seemed like he was bargaining with God in his head and had finally been given permission to speak his heart out. He was begging God to help us with such a passion. He was nearly a teenager by then and it was amazing to listen to him speak that way. He went on to apologize to God for any of his sins, and asked for forgiveness. He also continued to just beg God to change our situation and to help us go back to our house. That day I realized that my son was growing up and becoming a young man. Before then I hadn't truly realized how he had been carrying all our problems on his shoulders just like Amin and I. We were all so touched by his prayer that no one said anything for a few minutes after he was finished. Mrs. Fiet finally ended the prayer by simply thanking God for everything that he had done for us. Everyone went back downstairs after we had calmed down a bit, but my mind still couldn't get off my dream. In my heart, I was still waiting and hoping that something would happen because the day wasn't over yet. The second hand on the clock was extra loud that day, and with every tick I saw my hope of a breakthrough fading away. Then shortly after she had left Mrs. Fiet came back upstairs. She looked like she had good news.

"Cor has heard from Helen at the refugee office and she needs to meet with you tomorrow," she explained. I asked her what it was about, but she didn't know. I agreed to meet with her the next day, and began to wonder if this was the news I had been waiting for. Could it be? During the last possible moments of the 40th day had God worked another miracle? I didn't know what to think. My head was spinning, so I tried pushing it out of my mind until I could find out the next morning.

CHAPTER 17

I had been patiently waiting for news, any news at all, but I had not expected to be summoned to the refugee office so abruptly. Shortly thereafter, Helen from the immigration office called and asked to speak with me directly. She explained that she had reached out to several refugee organizations to get their advice on our case. They had been working directly with the City Council of Delft to try and form a plan to save us from deportation. Like I explained before, in the Netherlands, local government is given quite a bit of control of what goes on within their cities. Even though the immigration police had been given our deportation order, there may have been a chance that the City Council could help form a plan that could help us. She then explained that it was crucial that I come meet with her alone at her office the next morning, without Amin or anyone else.

I became very worried about going there alone, and I asked her if she could tell me over the phone. She apologized and said that she couldn't do it over the phone and that it must be in-person or by official letter, but since we were not living at our home any more this was the only way. I asked her why I had to come by myself and she told me that there was nothing to be worried about. She said that if there was any danger she would never have asked me to come meet with her. I was still nervous, but after all that she had done for us, I trusted Helen's word. I agreed to meet with her the next morning and hung up.

I was feeling very good that night because I had cried my heart out that day and released a huge amount of pent up emotion and frustration. God had been there with me all along and after my crying my prayer session that night I felt so much lighter and at ease. I had no fear whatsoever about what was going to happen the next day. Later, Amin came home with Cor and Pastor Blenk. They themselves had heard that Helen wanted to meet with me alone and were worried about my safety. They contacted the lawyers that the church had hired to help us and they assured Amin, Cor and the Pastor that I would not be in any danger by going to meet Helen.

Even after the assurance they got from their lawyers, the three of them had a lot to talk about before my trip to the immigration office the next day. They were busy that night making plans in case something went wrong. It was decided that there would be a few people watching over me from a distance and if anything happened, or if they wanted to take me to another location, these other people would somehow interfere to get me away to safety. More than anything they were worried that there may have been a plan to capture me to lure Amin into custody.

Mrs. Fiet and her husband were always wonderful islands of strength and wisdom no matter what chaos was going on around them, and this time was no different. They tried to calm Amin, Cor and Pastor Blenk down by reminding them of how amazing it was that we were able to escape from the immigration police the way that we did, and that we mustn't lose faith in God's protection and plan. Then Mrs. Fiet asked us all to pray, "Instead of letting all this negativity get the better of us, why don't we all sit down and pray for their continued safety? There are many of here and we should use that to our advantage. Prayers are even more powerful when two or more are gathered in His name."

Her words touched everyone and they realized she was right. We all prayed together and then they all left for the night, and we all went to sleep in our beds very easily without any worry in our minds. I had such a good night's rest that Amin didn't want to wake me up for breakfast or even to send the kids to school. He took care of the kids for me and got them ready for school all on his own. That night Mrs. Fiet's words reminded all of us to have faith in God and His miracles. Though he was still concerned for my safety, even Amin was feeling lighter that morning. Our prayer the night before reminded me of many stories from the Bible.

Stories of God's miracles from the Old Testament until the Book of Revelations. All we must do is have faith in Him and he will never forsake us. When God promised the Israelites that he'd take them out of bondage in Egypt there were many that lost faith along the journey, but always God sent a messenger to remind them of His love, and to remind them that He was in control. This same notion can be seen repeatedly all the way through the New Testament as well. Ultimately it reminded me that there is no need while we are in Christ, to worry about things like death or prison because no matter what happens we have His love and are a part of His plan.

That morning when I finally did wake up, I was filled with energy and was in especially good spirits. I spent some time in my morning devotions to God and then got ready to head to the refugee office. Mrs. Fiet's home was in the middle of the city on a canal that had a bridge over to the other side. The refugee office was on the south side of the city about five to seven minutes by bike, and I'd have to cross the bridge on my way to the other side of town. I left the house on Mrs. Fiet's bike and crossed the little bridge over the canal without any fear at all. I was feeling very confident in my safety and my purpose, even though I hadn't been able to move freely through the city by myself for some time. I finally arrived just down the street from the refugee office, and there was a large hill leading up to the office. I got off the bike and started to walk up the hill. As I walked I began thinking to myself that whatever happened, or what was told to me at the refugee office, I would look at it as a sign from God. I couldn't be afraid of what the outcome might be. I was determined to have faith and stay strong in the Lord.

I was lost in my thoughts when suddenly I noticed someone in the window waving at me trying to get my attention. When I got closer I saw that it was Helen. With hand signals, she tried to tell me that everything was good and to hurry up and come upstairs. I started to walk faster and before I knew it I was upstairs in her office. As soon as Helen saw me face-to-face she hugged me and said, "I am so very happy to see you!" She told me that I was a very strong woman and though she couldn't imagine the incredibly difficult times I'd been through; she was happy to say that she had good news for me that day.

Before she said anything, I told her, "I know you going to give me some good news today. I can say with all confidence that I know that you are going to tell me that we can move back to our house! I have no doubt in that because God has shown that to me in a vision."

She looked at me and was obviously very confused. She then asked me if someone else had told me this news? I told her simply, "Yes, God told me."

Again, she looked very confused. I went on to explain, "When you put all of your trust and faith in God Helen, you can see how great His miracles can be."

She acknowledged what I had said but still looked as though she didn't quite believe it. Then she continued to explain the details of what had been going on. She explained that the immigration police had apparently only been given deportation papers for Amin, not for me or the children, and because the house was in my name it was still there empty waiting for our return. She then said that it would be safe for the children and myself to go back to our home. Amin would have to wait for the lawyers to try and reopen his case by claiming a hardship based on his separation from his family. The whole-time Helen was talking and explaining all of this to the last detail I couldn't hear anything because all I was doing was thanking God for fulfilling his promises to us, and for not forsaking us.

I felt at the time that we had truly experienced God's favor. I had such a joy in my heart knowing what wonderful miracles can come through faithfulness in Christ. I wished that I had believed in Christ sooner so I could have experienced even more of His miracles that He had given to His children. I decided right then and there that I would never waste a day in my life, and that if only to experience more of God's love it would be reason enough to keep living and spreading His word.

I was deep in thought when I felt Helen's hand upon my shoulders. She asked me if I was okay and I smiled at her and said, "I am amazed by God's love and provision."

She could see the immense joy and excitement that was bubbling just under the surface within me. She then said, "I can see how happy you are. Why don't you go home and tell Amin about the good news? Just remember that only you and the children can return now until we can reopen Amin's case."

I thanked Helen and gave her a huge hug before saying goodbye. I then got back on the bike to head back to our little attic refuge. That little attic that had witnessed so many of my tears and prayers, and that would now be a place of joy and gratitude with this good news I was about to share with everyone.

When Mrs. Fiet opened the door, and saw the calmness in my eyes and face she immediate said, "You must have great news!"

I told her that God had heard our prayers, and I hugged her like I had never hugged her before. It was so touching and amazing to me that she had could always hold me close with the warmth of her love and compassion. Even through all the hardships and problems, she was always there, steady with her kind words of wisdom. I told her quickly what had happened because I knew Amin was upstairs waiting to hear what had gone on. I then raced up the stairs and immediately began to tell Amin everything. I told him how God's protection had been upon our family and how my dream and God's promise became true that day. We were both so happy, but I could also see that Amin was a little deflated because he knew that he couldn't come back with us. How could the kids and I go back to a house that we had shared as a family knowing that Amin was still in hiding on his own? Right then and there Amin and I went on our knees and started to thank God for his miraculous provision on our family. I then asked God to please allow us all to be together. We had gone through everything together, and I begged Him to please let us be by each other's side from now on as well.

Mrs. Fiet contacted Cor right away after I had gone upstairs, and gave him the good news. It spread through the church quickly after that, and everyone was amazed at this turn around in our decision. They were all so thankful. They believed that now 50% of the danger had been removed and the other 50% of danger remained until Amin's case was settled. We didn't think like that however; we were confident that we were 100% under God's protection and we had faith that God would not do a job halfway. If he started something he was going to finish it, and keep our family not only safe but together as well.

We decided to not tell the children yet. They had been at school when I returned that day and we wanted it to be a surprise. So, on Wednesday of that week I decided to go over to the house and start cleaning up so everything would be ready when we returned. I told Ida about my plan and asked her to bring the kids over after they got out of school early. Then we'd surprise them with the news and get them to help clean. Mrs. Fiet gave me a few cleaning supplies and I took the spare key I had kept for our old house. I went over to the house on the tram and stood in front of the door for a few moments. I put the key inside the keyhole and opened the door. and walked in. I immediately got down on my knees and started to pray, thanking God repeatedly. I also then anointed the house in the name of the Father, Son and the Holy Spirit and asked that God bring His protection over our house.

A few minutes later the kids arrived and were so surprised and happy. We started to clean the house together. They were even happy to clean their rooms! They were sparked with this excited energy and cleaned furiously into the evening! It was finally time to head back to Mrs. Fiet's house and the kids asked why we had to go back. I explained that we will come back to live in our house when the time is right. I had promised Mrs. Fiet that we come back to stay with her until all our affairs were sorted, and we could be positive that it was safe to return. Besides, we had so much to thank God for in the meantime. It was time to give thanks and make our preparations to come back to the home we had loved so much. The kids and I then prayed one last time before leaving. We thanked God again and asked him not only to protect our family and our house, but to help us use that house for His glory and His purpose. All our problems had not disappeared, but we were confident that God would continue to give us the provision that he saw fit, and we would continue to be blessed. We just wanted to make sure that if we could continue to live in that house, that we committed to using it to honor God.

The next day our neighbor called Cor. She had promised to let us know if anything suspicious happened around our house, and sure enough she told Cor that there were people from the city that were trying to use their universal keys to get in. By some stroke of luck, they were not able to enter the home though. The City had keys to every home that they were giving to the refugees and they had the right to enter those homes anytime they wanted to, but mostly in cases of an emergency. When we had fled our home in early December there were government agents that arrived with their keys and walked right in looking to arrest us. So, we were surprised to hear that all our neighbors had witnessed the fact that the people from the city weren't able to get in even with their keys this time. They even tried to break down the door, but to no avail. When we heard this news, we were shocked and thought that it might have been a set up to get us to go back home so they could arrest us. However, Cor learned from the neighbor that this wasn't the case at all. The people from the city had come over to make sure the place was fit for habitation because some things had been broken by the immigration police the night that we left. Yet they still could not get their keys to work. For me this was a sign from God that once we had anointed our home, and prayed to God to cover it with His protection, and to use our house according to His purpose, that no man could break through that.

Three days passed and we still weren't living in our old home. Helen called me and asked, "Why haven't you all gone back to the house yet?

I told her that I couldn't go back without my husband Amin, and if Amin couldn't go yet there was no point in the rest of us going. Helen told me not to worry because Amin's case was much stronger now, and the lawyers believed that things would be settled relatively quickly now. Apparently, my health issues, and the health issues that the children had suffered were a reason to claim a hardship. It was so strange to me that problems caused by the stress of the long waiting process were now reasons that we might get our case expedited. It was very ironic to me. Truthfully though, by that time my hip pain had gotten quite bad by that point, and I needed a major-medical procedure. This would only be possible if I was granted permanent citizenship. Luckily my physical therapist wrote us a letter explaining the gravity of my health situation and pleaded to have our case resolved as soon as possible because I may not have could walk if I did not receive the medical care I so desperately needed. They also wrote another letter concerning Omid's nosebleeds and MJ's headaches.

The lawyers hoped that this pressure along with the threat of legal action should anything happen with our medical conditions, would help speed along the approval process and at least help make it safe for Amin to come back to the house.

Helen was very positive, but she urged me to return to the house without Amin for a time, "I need you to go back home so we can show the court that you can't take care of the kids by yourself and that the kids can't stay away from their father for a long time. We can show that this distance is causing emotional damage to all of you day-by-day. Don't worry, you'll all be reunited very soon."

The church leaders also agreed with Helen, and urged us to return to the house without Amin for a short time. I was excited to get back home so we could begin living our normal lives again, but I had gotten so comfortable and dependent on Mrs. Fiet and her husband that it saddened me a little to leave. They had shown us love and compassion in a way that we had never felt before. They opened our eyes to the true depth of Christ's love. They showed us that they would do anything for us, even open their home to complete strangers, and comfort us in our darkest hours of despair. When we cried, they had cried with us, and it would be very difficult to be away from these kind souls. Mrs. Fiet was a great role model for me and I learned based on what the Bible says in the book of Acts that believers are united by doing God's work, and we were truly united under His purpose. They lived His word every day in their own lives.

We left their house that day with many tears and plenty of hugs. I couldn't ever fully express the immense level of gratitude I felt for these amazing people. It wouldn't be easy to leave, especially with Amin still there, but it was time to move on. The children all hugged Mrs. Fiet intensely and promised her that they'd come back and visit her whenever they could, and of course to see Amin whenever possible. Mrs. Fiet promised me that she'd take good care of Amin, and told me not to worry about him, and said that she was sure we'd be reunited sooner than we thought.

After a short trip by car we arrived at our old home and made our way up to the door. Ida had come with us and we were all so excited to be back in that familiar place. I had a strange feeling as soon as I entered the house though. It was almost as if I could feel that the house was under God's protection. I was filled with a huge sense of peace.

From that day on I also tried to do things that I thought would please God. I prayed every day for God to show me what he wanted me to do to serve Him, and to open the right doors so I could serve Him in every way that I could. Of course, I also begged Him to send Amin back home to us so we could serve Him together. Luckily God did hear my prayers, and in addition to all the amazing doors that were about to happen, He brought Amin back to us just 10 days after we first arrived. We were finally reunited and safe all together in our home. It was indescribable, the feeling of happiness we felt being together again in that place. After that it was like we were a new family. Our entire lifestyle was born again in service of the Lord. God had truly changed our lives.

After much prayer and many discussions with the board members of the church we decided to have bible studies at our house in Farsi so we could spread the good news of Christ to more of our own countrymen and women. Surprisingly in that little city of Delft there were over 1500 Iranians living there, and we couldn't wait to spread God's word to them. We knew that many of them were in the same position we had been in, and were lost in this new country and culture, and Jesus was the only answer to truly finding a peaceful refuge. Forced, the pastor from Almere even agreed to come to our Bible study every month to preach. It was a glorious time when we could all see God working miracles through His children.

I would also attend month bible studies twice a month at Ida's house with the regular women's group in Dutch. I started to study the word of God deeper and I realized how little I still knew about God and his love. I still had a million questions and loved learning more and more. The love of Christ was in my heart, and I wanted to soak up all that I could.

CHAPTER 18

Our lives had changed spiritually but the health of myself and the children was still not good. Omid was still having his nosebleeds quite frequently, and after completing a few of the initial procedures he continued to have them. We took him to a specialist and they concluded that one of the main veins in his nose was torn. Because of this he would continue to have ever nose bleeds unless they took more drastic actions. They decided to first attempt to freeze the vein, and if that did not work, they would have to try and cauterize it. Omid had constant nightmares during this time and some nights he would wake up and come to my room and ask me to pray with him. He was losing a lot of sleep and we were worried that this would make his immune system even more week to deal with the nose bleeds. We discussed it with his doctor and he explained that there was little we could do about the nightmares until our situation had been settled, and that it was normal for a child to have nightmares when they are under stress. We decided to go forward with the first procedure to freeze the vein in his nose and decided to have him sleep in our room for a while just so he would feel as secure and safe as possible. Luckily after the first procedure to fix the vein in his nose, the nosebleeds did start to let up and Omid began to feel more at ease.

MJ's headache was also getting more serious during this time. It seemed to me that every time he had a severe headache, he would react by getting very angry. It was difficult to tell whether this was because he was being a normal teenager, or because there was something off in his brain because of his seizure condition, and it was being amplified by our stressful living situation. There were also times that he would watch over me with fear and anxiety. I think as he was growing into a young man, he saw it as his responsibility to take care of us. One Sunday we were coming back from the Persian church and he was very quiet.

He seemed exhausted so I asked him if something had happened. He said no and told me that he was just a little tired. I assumed it was because of the long car ride and left it at that. When we got home he was feeling better and he had his dinner. Then later that evening he went to bed. For some reason Omid kept asking if he could sleep in MJ's room. So much so that finally we gave in and just said yes. They both went to sleep without any incidents after that. Later that night after we'd all been sleeping; Omid came running into our bedroom crying.

He said, "Mom wake up! MJ is Dead!"

For a second I thought he was having nightmares again, and like always I hugged him to try and calm him down. This time was different though, he pushed himself off and took my hand and kept telling me to hurry because MJ was dying. I realized then that he was wide awake and by then I could hear noises coming from MJ's room. I jumped of my bed wide awake, and work up Amin. We both ran to MJ's room.

Now that many years have passed, I still can't forget that moment. I get goose bumps and my eyes fill up with tears when I remember what I saw when I got to MJ that night. We walked in to find MJ shaking very badly, and his hands and feet were lurching violently all over the place. His eyes were rolled back into his head and his crooked mouth was white with foam. Right away Amin held him very tightly but he could control him by himself. I was trying to hold his legs but it seemed like they were made from metal and were moving very forcefully. There was no way I could hold on. The only thing that came to my mind was to run bare footed to our neighbor's house, whom we were very close with, because she worked as a nurse in the surgery wing at the hospital. I pounded on their front door and was crying very loudly trying to get them to wake up and come to the door. They were still half asleep when they came to the door, and they saw my face covered in tears they could tell that something was horribly wrong. They didn't even wait for me to say anything. Instead they just ran, also bare footed, towards our apartment. She rushed into MJ's room and immediately realized the gravity of the situation, and called 911 right away. It was only a few minutes until the ambulance arrived, but in the meantime, they were telling her over the phone what to do so MJ wouldn't stop breathing before they got there.

Amin was constantly praying for him the entire time, and asking Christ to save our son. Omid was sitting in a corner of the room softly crying and needing someone to hug him as well. For someone to get him out of this nightmare that had become reality after he woke up. Our neighbor's husband hugged Omid and told him it would be all right. He looked up and motioned to me to let me know that we would take Omid to their house so he wouldn't have to witness what was going on.

The ambulance finally arrived and the paramedics could get the seizure under control with medications. MJ had stopped the violent part of the seizure, but he wasn't fully conscious. He just stared up at the ceiling as if he weren't there. I put my clothes on and rushed with them to the hospital. After a few tests, we learned that MJ was in a coma. After completing an MRI, they explained that the portion of MJ's brain that had sustained the trauma when he was a baby was now growing. This was putting pressure on his skull and was affecting the brain. They moved him to the ICU to monitor his situation, and hooked him up to a lot of machines. There were many doctors there just for him. After much discussion, they decided to keep him hooked up to the machines for 72 hours in case he had another major seizure. It could be life threatening at that point, so they wanted to know immediately if something was starting. The doctors continued to perform all sorts of test on him throughout the night. MJ just lay there perfectly calm and motionless, with no signs of the son we knew and loved.

God knows what I went through in those few hours, and the only thing I could do was to pray for him. I talked to God and begged Him once again to put me through test and trials instead of my son. All the doctors and nurses who kept going in and out of his room tried very hard to comfort me and calm me down. They told me to be sure to have a positive attitude while I was in his room, and to talk to him so they could see if my voice could stir any reawakening of his memory and brain function. Of course, I did what they told me to, and talked to MJ every moment I was in his room. The only sign of life that MJ showed while I was talking to him were the drops of tears that flowed down his cheeks, but still he never said a word. It seemed like with every drop of tears my heart broke more and more. It was very difficult to stay strong and keep myself from breaking down in his presence. was coming out of my chest and I was holding myself back from crying.

One of the specialists was very kind and loving, and encouraged me to stay strong for MJ. He told me that I must keep talking to him, and that it would help stimulate healing in the brain. So, I did. I started talking to him nonstop. I talked to him about all the good memories I had of him growing up, and of our time in Holland. I talked to him about all the plans I had for him for the future, and I talked to him about his brother and how much he missed him. Each time I talked to MJ, I felt in my heart that he was hearing me. I held his little hands in mine every time and looked for signs of movement. For a long time, I saw nothing, and his little fingers just sat limp in my hand, but eventually I noticed there was a little movement beginning to happen. Finally, after being up most of the night, he squeezed my hand back a little. It was a small sign of progress, but it was a good sign nonetheless. I felt so thankful for this little bit of hope. It was a very hard night for us and like every night there is always a morning. If there were not a morning after every night, then what are we supposed to do with all the nightmares from the nights before?

I was feeling very tired and was missing my mother very much. It was during times like this that I felt her absence the most. All I wanted at that moment was for her to be there so I could lay my head on her chest, and so she could tell me that what had happened the night before was just a nightmare. MJ squeezed my hand once again and I came back to my senses. I asked God to make me stronger so I could be the rock in my son's life, and show him that we'd get through this together. In the meantime, Amin arrived at the hospital and walked into the room. I could see that he was completely broken. His eyes were red and all puffed up from crying all night. When I saw his face, I became worried that maybe all of this had been too much for him. He looked like the night had taken a toll on him.

He came into the room and, "Hello".

MJ heard his voice right away and he started to cry. With a very weak voice he called to his Father, "Dad...dad."

The doctors were all very excited to see the effect that Amin had had on MJ. They all agreed that the real danger had passed, and now we just needed to continue to encourage him to speak more and more.

Amin began telling me everything that had happened after we left for the hospital. He said that our neighbors had taken care of Omid and even kept him busy until it was time for school. Then our good friends Cor and Ida had could come over to take Omid to school so Amin would not have to leave the hospital. Both of us were very tired and now that MJ's prognosis looked positive, we decided that we must also get some rest. MJ's room was large and very clean so we thought it would be easiest for us to just setup camp there and take shifts looking over MJ. I had been limping around because I must have put too much pressure on my hip when I was running to the neighbors' house, and my hip was causing me a lot of pain. So, the nurse brought an extra bed in for me to lie down on.

MJ and I were lying next to each other and Amin was there looking after both of us. I began to think about how lucky I was to have him, and began thanking God for putting Amin in my life. He was always by my side every moment. Even when I went through all the pain with my hip, he would sit next to me and go through it with me. He always tried to take the weight off my shoulders. He was much more than just my husband; he had become my best and most trusted friend. It was a huge cry from where we had started in our marriage, and I knew that it was a miracle that our partnership had could grow and flourish like it had.

MJ looked very weak and tired with bruises all over his body from the violent seizure, but at least it appears he was beginning to heal. According to the doctors, he was progressing very fast, but still after 3 days he had to be hooked to all those machines. In the mornings after Amin would give Omid his breakfast and take him to school, he would come to the hospital and then leave in the evening to pick him up from Ida's house. Then he'd stay the night at our house with Omid, and I'd stay the night with MJ. I only slept when Amin would come during the day. I just couldn't rest without knowing one of us was watching over his condition. Finally, after a week in the hospital the doctors said that he was well enough to return home. They explained that he'd need to come in once every two weeks for checkups over the next six months, and that he'd need to be on constant medication until he was finished growing. They said that the scars from his brain surgery were stretching and it could cause him to have seizures for years until his brain had stopped growing. Our lives would be a little different once we brought him home, but we were all just thankful that we were able to bring him home at all.

When he came home he was talking, but moving and living in slow motion. We tried to make the house more peaceful and I also paid more attention to the kids' nutrition to make sure he got all the right vitamins. He was so weak though that he still didn't talk much or even has an appetite to eat for quite some time. According to the doctors the healing process would depend on a lot of things. For example; living a normal childhood without any problems was one way to minimize the trauma to his brain. This event had made us realize that we were not the only ones that were under pressure because of our immigration status. The kids were also under intense mental pressure and hardship because of it. We saw this manifest with their health issues, and we tried very hard after that to shield both from it as much as possible.

It had been a few days since MJ had been released from the hospital and we asked his doctors if it was okay for us to send him back to school so he wouldn't be home alone all the time, and they said yes. He had to take medications twice a day and his teachers were so supportive of him once he came back. We tried to be strong even with all the problems and issues that we were facing. We continued to go once a month to the Persian church and with the help of our friends in our home church, we decided to invite the Iranians from the refugee center closest to us to come with us to the Persian church. Our Dutch friends helped us drive everyone to there, and were excited to help us get the word out to the Persian people living in the camps.

For the most part, life in a refugee camp is very boring and I felt like people may be more open to hear the truth of God and His word because they had little else to keep them busy. We were so pleased to see that every time we'd visit a camp and talk about the love of Christ, we could see how some of the people we spoke to had a lightness inside of them that they had lost somewhere along their journey. After our visits, we would then invite them to our home for Bible studies and to accompany us to the Persian church once a month in Almere. It was very rewarding to share the good news of Christ to people from our own country and try to help them find their new lives in Christ like we had. It was also our way of working for the Lord and giving thanks for everything that we had been given.

Even with all our work with the church, it still didn't feel like we were living a normal life though because we after four years of living there we still didn't have any answers in regards to our immigration status. The church had hired two very good lawyers and still no answers. It was so frustrating to not know what our future would look like, and to not be able to get real jobs and build a foundation for our family. At that time, Social Services was not paying us our salaries either because it took a while for that all to start up again after we were in hiding. So, the church decided to find Amin an under the table, paying job so he could go to work just like everyone else on a daily basis and have pride in taking care of his family.

I also continued to go to college and after we got back to our house Rima even came back to live with us for a while so we could finish college together. At the college, I met many more new friends, and one of them was a young African lady by the name of Sophie. She was a very kind young girl and before I had quit smoking she and I would go out to have cigarettes together while we talked. When I returned after we were in hiding, we picked up right where we left off even though I was no longer a smoker. Sophie would always tell me about her dreams and how she wanted to bring her daughter from Columbia to the Netherlands. She was a very beautiful girl but you could see through her eyes that she was struggling with many problems. She had and intense sadness about her. She was talking about her life in a very positive way, but always at the end of our conversations she would have tears coming down her face. Still she would never mention her problems.

One day I could tell that she wasn't herself at all throughout class. She knew that I had quit smoking, so right after class she ran downstairs to smoke her cigarette. This way she would be done with it by the time I walked out, and we'd have a chance to talk. That day she told me how she has gotten her citizenship in the Netherlands. She had married a 65-year-old man and now her husband was taking full advantage of the situation and not treating her right. He forced her to work at a restaurant washing dishes and he'd keep all the money she made. She didn't know how to speak the language, so she was doing whatever she was told. When she showed me her hands they were full of blisters and there were some areas that had bad burned as well.

She told me at the restaurant they give her all the heavy jobs but that she refused to complain. She said that every minute of every day she was thinking of her daughter and how to get her to the Netherlands. Simon her husband had told her that if she wanted her daughter with her she'd have to work double so there'd be enough to save money for the lawyer. It was very hard for her to do because she also had to pay for his living expenses as well.

She told me that she was working seven days a week, and that after she paid all the bills at the house she only had a very small amount to save for her daughter's lawyer. I could see in her eyes that she was a loving and caring mother but that this husband was taking full advantage of her both physically and financially. He was putting so much pressure on her that she would never succeed in bringing her daughter to be with her in the Netherlands. She had to be married for 5 years to be even can apply for her daughter to come and her marriage was only three years old at that time. She had no choice but to keep doing exactly what he said. Her life from morning to afternoon was filled with college classes and after that she would go straight to the restaurant and work until midnight. Besides me she didn't have any other friends and she never had a chance to talk with anyone about her problems. I could see that she was very lonely and physically exhausted from the physical labor.

We became very close friends so I invited her and her husband to our house for dinner one night. She was very happy to receive my invitation and told me that it had been over a year since she had dinner around a proper table. She told me that her husband would have to meet me first before he would decide whether or not they could come over. She asked me to stay behind after class that day so I could meet her husband when he came to pick her up and I agreed.

When I finally saw, him I felt bad for her. He was a very serious man and on top of that he was over 65 years old. In the little time that we had to meet he was evaluating me and asking a how list of questions about my family and our immigration status. After we talked for a few minutes he said that he remembered us from reading our story in the newspaper and on television. After this he felt more comfortable and accepted our invitation for dinner. Sophie had to request a night off so they could come over to our house, and after a few nights they came over. Her husband started to ask Amin and I questions based on what he had seen in the news in regards to our immigration status. He looked at Sophie and would say things like, "See how lucky you are? It is so hard to get citizenship in this country."

We knew this was all part of his plan to make his wife fearful of him, and to make her feel like it would be worse if she left him. He was very serious toward his wife and at times it seemed like she wasn't even there or like she was not human. I felt really bad for her and wanted to tell her husband, "Sir the years of slavery are over. This is the 20th century!" But Amin was looking at me all night trying to make sure I didn't say anything to upset him.

The kids liked Sophie and tried to stay with her the whole time they were there. It didn't take very long for us to understand what kind of relationship these two had. He was insulting his wife constantly and I could see that Sophie was embarrassed. The main reason I didn't speak up about his horrible behavior was because I didn't want to make her feel more ashamed then she already did. I had been praying for her before they came over, but after Amin observed Simon's behavior we decided to pray for Sophie even more seriously so God could touch Simon's heart and soften it toward his wife. Of course, we also prayed very hard for God to help bring Sophie's daughter to be with her mother.

A few days after the dinner Sophie came to me crying and said that she was tired of living with Simon and that she couldn't do it anymore. I asked her if they had gotten into a fight but she said no. She explained that she had just realized that he didn't care about her or her daughter and that he hadn't done anything to help reunite them.

"From the very first day he has been lying to me about hiring a lawyer and working on bringing my daughter here," she said.

I asked her what she going to do now, and she said she was planning on divorcing him. I told her to not make hasty decisions, and that she had put up with him for three long years. I encouraged her to pray about it and ask God for his wisdom. To pray for God to touch Simon's heart and make him see the errors of his ways. I told her to take her time before deciding because once it was done she'd start from the beginning and wouldn't have her citizenship anymore.

I saw how damaged her hands were, and I kissed them. I told her that her hands were holy in the eyes of God because of how hard she was working for her daughter. "God will not let your hands and heart be empty. Pray about it, and let him guide you."

Right then and there I started to pray for her and asked Christ to give her peace and comfort. I also prayed with her for her husband, Simon and for God to touch his heart. After prayer, I saw that she looked different and more peaceful so I asked her try to work a little less and to take better care of herself.

"Just remember, you can do these things while you are a citizen of the country but if you get divorced it will be much harder for you to bring your daughter here. Go home with peace in your heart, and rest a little. Maybe when you get home your husband will look at you differently and finally see what kind of mistake he has been making," I told her.

Sophie was very grateful that she had someone to talk to about all of this. That day she decided to take my advice, and to demand that she work less and take better care of herself. She turned all her focus, 100% on bringing her daughter to live with her. Over time her husband got used to her not working as much and began to give in on a lot of things. It appears he had finally understood that she was the only one willing to put up with his negative attitude, and he realized that he was lucky that she had chosen to stay with him. After that he agreed to be more proactive in helping bring her daughter to live with them, and after just a few months she came to the Netherlands. We talked every single day we saw each other in school, and I could see the light that her daughter had brought to her life. I was so happy for her. She stayed with Simon for quite a while after that but eventually things began to go back to the way they were before. By that time, however, she had her permanent citizenship and finally divorced him. She also purchased a share of the restaurant she was working in and continued to take care of herself and her daughter. She was a true example of the strength and determination I saw in so many refugees, and it was inspiring to see how God was working in their lives.

I was still in contact with Mrs. Fiet during that time and she knew that it was in my heart to help other Iranian immigrants. So, she introduced me to an Iranian woman who was also struggling with her immigration status. She was alone and she lived in the busiest part of the town and she had rented a room above a nightclub. Mrs. Fiet was explaining to me about her situation was very bad and she also had health issues. and, her health issues and she asked me to go visit her. I went to visit her for the first time, her name was Farah and she was looking at everything with negative eyes life or people. She was explaining to me when she was living in the refugee camp she met this Iranian guy and they like each other and after a while they got married. Her mother in law came to the Netherlands to visit her son and her new daughter in law and when she saw her she did not like her at all and she forced her son to divorce even though her son loved Farah he couldn't say anything and disobey her mother. He was helping Farah secretly though and even the place she was living at he got it for her so she won't be homeless. Farah had met Mrs. Fiet through the church and because Farah couldn't speak that well Dutch Mrs. Fiet had asked me to help her however I can.

She poured out her heart and talked about how she is broken spiritually and doesn't have any hope at all. First thing I told her was about the love of Christ and she had heard something about the love of Christ at the church but because of her language she didn't get it all the way and it seemed like she wanted to know about Christ.

I had a Persian Bible and I gave it to her and I told her where to start reading. I tried to go visit her once a week so she won't be lonely, after some visits I saw some changes in her attitude and I thought it was weird and I would tell myself it is probably because of her situation. The meeting I would have with her weekly she would complain about everyone and everything and I was trying always to shift her mindset and thoughts to something else so she can think about the past little less. I would at times ask her to come over to our house and after couple times that she came over I realized that she didn't even like Rima who was living with us at that time. She would always talk bad about her and was trying to turn me against her but I did not allow her to do that and I asked her when you come over to my house I don't like for you to talk about other people or talk bad about them and she said okay. After a few weeks hanging out with her and talking with her I found out that she had bad pains in her shoulders and in her spine and she needed medical attention. We took her to a specialist and after some test the doctor said it's because she has big boobs and her bone structure is so small her body can't handle carrying the weight of her boobs so she had to make her boobs smaller but she was worried that after surgery there is no one to take care of her. I decided to discuss this matter with Mrs. Fiet and Amin and we concluded for her to come straight to our house after her surgery so I can take care of her but it was kind of hard because we had given a room to Rima and now we had to make the kids room ready for her and the kids would have been at that time without a room. But Rima said that she will room up with the kids and the kids loved it because they like her and were always happy when she was around. Me and her ex-husband took her to the hospital for her surgery and after surgery she had to stay there for another 3 days and after that me and her ex-husband brought her back to our house. Her ex was a very nice gentleman and he was very thankful that we were helping her out. Because of the surgery it was hard for Farah to move her hands so I had to do everything for her. 10 days had passed since her surgery and we had to take her for a check-up, the doctors were happy with her progress and they told her that she needs to use her own hands now like eating her own food brushing her own teeth and even taking her own shower and that it has been almost 2 weeks since her surgery and now she can do everything on her own because her wounds were healing very fast. She was still living with us for another 3 weeks and every with every opportunity she tried to make me against Rima and stir something between us and I would ask Rima to humble herself and not say anything but it had gotten very far that she tried to kick Rima out of our home and she told me if you don't kick Rima out of your house I will leave.

First I tried to talk to her with love and finish this whole drama but it got to a point that I was fed up with it as well so I contacted her ex-husband and explained everything to him and told him to pick her up and take him to his own house because she is better now and she can do her own chores. He told me that when his parents came from Iran to visit him she did the exact same thing to him and it was because she wouldn't get along with his mother and it had gotten to a point that she told me its either me or you mother that can stay here so make up your mind. One time we got in such a big fight that the neighbors had called the police on us and because of all that we ended up getting divorced. Now I realized what the main reason was for his divorce by what I heard from her ex and what I had seen these past few weeks. That night when he came to pick her up she was shocked that why she had to leave our home she was trying all along to have Rima kick out. That was a very bad night she started to yell at Rima and curse me saying that you're throwing me out because of this girl who is a nobody, she even cursed my children out and her ex was trying to calm her down but it wasn't working out at all because she would raise her voice even more. Finally, with a calm voice and with respect I asked her now that you are feeling better and for you now to be around Rima is good for you to go to his house for a few days so you can get calm and get some peace because after that surgery being angry is not good for you and you seem weak now and you need to rest. I had gotten her bag ready and secretly I told her ex to take her as soon as possible to his house and try not to leave her alone tonight. He was very embarrassed and he was being very thankful to us and took Farah with him. When all this happened, Amin wasn't home and when he came home I told him what had happened and he was very upset and told me that I should not have any contact with her anymore and we need to let Mrs. Fiet know about what had happened so she can be careful as well. By the time I would try to contact Mrs. Fiet and tell her what had happened Farah had already contacted her that night and talked to her with the little Dutch she knew and with sadness and crying that Sara kicked me out of the house in the middle of the night while I am still sick.

First I was very upset but like always God knows when to give me peace he has said in his word there are time that if you do good things to people they will answer all the things that you have done for them with bad attitude or talk bad about you and what is more sweeter and more peaceful then God's word. I was feeling bad for Farah so I talked to Mrs. Fiet and I asked her to talk to her ex in regards of her leaving our house or you could even ask Rima but Mrs. Fiet like always answered with wisdom and per the word of God let your Yes be yes and let your No be no and if you say that's not the way you had asked Farah to leave then I believe and there is no need for me to ask anyone else. First I was a little upset why no one saw or appreciated what I have done for her but again God knows when to talk to me and to paint a picture more clearly for me. in his word, it says "Be careful! When you do something good, don't do it in front of others so that they will see you. If you do that, you will have no reward from your Father in heaven. "When you give to those who are poor, don't announce that you are giving. Don't be like the hypocrites. When they are in the synagogues and on the streets, they blow trumpets before they give so that people will see them. They want everyone to praise them. The truth is, that's all the reward they will get. So, when you give to the poor, don't let anyone know what you are doing. Your giving should be done in private. Your Father can see what is done in private, and he will reward you. Matthew 6:1-4.

After that not only I had peace but I felt sorry for her as well so I asked Mrs. Fiet what can we do to help her out and after thinking about it a lot we couldn't come up with anything but only pray for her so God can touch Farah's heart and give her peace. When I would think about it I would see what kind of weird world we are living in we still had our own problems and God would still use us and test our patience and love towards others and it was always different scenarios or different people from Iranians to people from other nation and I believe one of the main reason for that was for us not to only look at what kind of problems we are going through but also pay attention to other people and care for them as well. I was trying with the people that God was putting in our path and who needed help and was seeking God's love to help them out with the help of the church. Since we had moved back into our home God was using us and our home in many ways. We were in contacts with the Iranian church all the time if it was taking the Iranians from the refugee camps to the church once a month or having once a month bible study at our own house and we were spreading God's love and his salvation to people who were seeking it. our home was a bridge kind of for Muslims to get to know Christ and I thank God that he had opened our home or should I say his home and was using us to serve other who wanted to get to know him.

There were always people who realized that they were sinners and wanted to become a believer in Christ. It had gotten to a point that we weren't only serving at one refugee camp but it was now a multiple refugee camps that we would go to and spread the good news and while we were always in prayers and asking God to open more refugee camps for us to go too he also showed us that we need to go back to our old refugee camp. It was hard for us to go back there because of all the good and bad memories we had there and there were also people from before that we knew there and we had gotten hurt from them a lot. I asked God to give me peace and wisdom when we go there so I would not hold anything against them for what they had done to me or my family in the past but to show love and share with them the treasure that God has given to us with them.

From the information, we had about Mehran and Shary was that they had been transferred out of that Refugee center and they had been placed into a home with a family of 3 which I knew they wouldn't be happy because they always wanted to be close to our home. We contacted Mehran and Shary and asked them if there are anyone from before left at that center and they said there is maybe a few Iranian families left but there are some new single Iranians there now. So, we tried to go visit the old Iranian families and through them get to know the new ones. I called one of the old families that we knew and told them that we would like to come and visit them and asked them what kind of food they liked and I would provide that for them so I made 3 types of their favorite meals and made enough for a crowd of 25 people. When we parked in front of the center all the memories I had from that place became new again. For a minute I was depressed but right away my mindset changed and I became happy because through all that hardship and problems and drama there we found an amazing treasure, which was worth experiencing and going through all what we went through at that center. With seeing some of our old friends at that center we were happy some of them had received their citizenship and they were waiting for a place to live and some they were still waiting for answers. The person who was in charge at that center when he heard we were there came and said hi and he was very happy as well that we came there to visit them and told us that he has been following our case through newspapers and television and he wishes us the best.

Also, the social worker that was working there came to see us and after we said our hellos she told us that she never thought we would be back at that place again with all the bad memories you guys had from here. I told her if God can forgive us from all the wrong things we do and our sins, who are we that we can't show the same love and forgiveness towards other people. She was very shocked with my response and with the way I was acting and said as far as I know you guys don't have your citizenship still but you seem so calm and peaceful why is that. So, in a short summary I gave her a small testimony with all the things that has happened to us and what kind of miracles God has done in our lives and this calmness and peace is also one his miracles. She would listen to every word I had to say and with a warm heart she told the cooks in the kitchen to set aside a meal for us as well. After we finished our meal with the social worker we went upstairs to the room of our friend and asked them to invite all the Iranian families there as well and that they are our guest for lunch that day. After lunch Amin and me had the privilege of meeting our old friends and meeting some new people at that center. It was a very nice day we talked and laughed the whole time and after everything we invited them to come to our home for one of our bible studies and if they like that we would take care of their transportation for coming to our house and leaving our house. When I saw that they were all curious I decided to share with them a little bit about our story how we met some Christian Dutch people and told them about December 4th of 1995 how God saved us through them form the immigration police, and when they saved us it opened our eyes and it was a start for our salvation and believing in Christ. Some of them were listening with a question mark on their forehead and some they tried to get more of the story by asking more questions. There was also a family in that room that didn't like us talking about that and was against it and with attitude they left the room and as soon as they left the room other people who were there stated to ask questions about the bible and church. We had brought a few bibles with us as well to give them out to whoever wanted one some they were so excited of having a bible in Farsi but some with a respect denied the gift we were giving them because they were fearful. I could understand those people so well because I used to be like them have fear and questions. That day we had talked a lot with a lot of people there some would talk about their problems there and other people they would say that they are happy for us because we don't have to live there and that we have our own place so we invited them if they ever feel depressed or they want to get away from the center they are always welcome at our house and they can stay a couple nights there to freshen up and get some peace. It was around evening time and we were about to leave when we saw a police officer coming after us from the social worker's office and the manager from the center and the officer asked us to go to the office of the manager.

We were shocked of what had happened that they came and picked us up like that so we hurried and went to the office of the manager and when we got there we saw the family that was against everything we were saying in that room. When they left the room with anger they had gone to the manager's office and telling him that we are causing trouble at the center and to kick us out but the manager knew us very well and didn't do anything about it and ignored them when they saw that he didn't do anything they went to the social worker and she ignored them as well and didn't do anything. With anger, they went to the police station and told them there are suspicious activities going on at the center and they fear for their safety because they are refugees and don't want any problems and that's why they had the police involved and the person who oversaw this whole this was Esi. The manager of the center and the social worker knew that we had prior problems with him they didn't do anything and they were trying to explain it to the police officer and told him that this complain is useless it's just a personal thing that they had in the past. The police office said because we have received a complaint we need to talk to Amin and Sara to make sure they are not putting anyone in danger or not doing any suspicious activities. After the police officer talked to us and to the other people in that room he found out that Esi had been insulting us not the other way around so he asked us if we would like to place a complain on him and open a case for him for insulting and accusing you guys. When I looked at him I felt really sorry for him and the only thing I told him you can always turn to God and ask for forgiveness and today we brought the good news for everyone come and save yourself from whatever you going through and feel the love and peace of God its beyond amazing it seemed like he heard me but I don't know if he heard me with open heart because the word of God says "he who has ears doesn't want to hear and he who has eyes doesn't want to see".

Therefore speak I to them in parables: because they seeing see not; and hearing they hear not, neither do they understand.
- Matthew 13:13

When the police officer saw how we acted towards Esi told him you got lucky that they didn't complaining or press charges on you otherwise it would have been bad for your immigration case. After this whole drama, the manager at the center and the social worker send us away with love and the other Iranians that witnessed all that apologized to us. After a full day of memories, we left the camp and when we got home we put Esi on our prayer list and started to pray for his salvation. We tried also to give the good news of Christ to all the Iranians we knew because we had received it for free and we are supposed to give it away for free. The people at college who knew me from before and had been following our case would ask me how your case is going now. Before I would answer them without any hope and would give them hopeless answers but after I became a follower of Christ my response was different I would tell them "if it's God's will for us to live in this country then he will open all the doors for us to stay here". They would tell me well he hasn't opened any new doors for you guys so what's his will for you guys. I would respond to them he must have a better place for us, they would ask me again if they deport you to Iran would you still say that's what God's will was. I would tell them I am surrendered to God and he knows what's best for me. They would ask me where do you get this faith from. After they asked me that question the Holy Spirit put in my heart that's the best opportunity to talk about Christ and plant a seed in their heart. I would tell them about how we got saved and God's love while we were going through all kinds of hardship and at the end I would tell them today is the day that God has put you in my path so we can have this conversation and you can hear about God's love. Some would listen with all their heart and would ask me for my address for bible studies and asking me if I can provide them a bible. Some would try to change the subject or tell me with respect that they are not interested.

CHAPTER 19

One day while in class I met a Persian woman who lived alone with her son. I don't know if she had always been in our class, but if she had been, I had never certainly never noticed her. I also did not recognize her from outside of class, but for some reason that day she caught my attention. I went up and introduced myself to her and learned that her name was Parvin. At first she tried to be very formal but when she found out that I also had a son who was six years old, she began to loosen up. I invited her to come over and have the kids play anytime that was good for her. She was very excited by the invitation, and she got my address right away and promised that she'd come over with her son very soon.

The first time she came over to our house, the kids clicked with each other right away and they started playing with each other like they'd always known each other. Her son's name was Sephr and I could tell he was her entire life. She was so happy that he and Omid hit it off. We had a very good day together that day and she didn't mention any of her personal life stories at all. However, she did ask me how long we had lived in the Netherlands. I began telling her our story, and eventually started to talk to her about the love of God, and this love had changed our lives. She asked me where it said that in the Koran about God's love. I told her very directly that I had not read about it in the Koran, nor was I aware of the Koran ever mentioning God's love at all, but that I had read it in the Holy Bible where Jesus Christ talks about God the Father's love of His children quite often.

She looked at me quizzically and then asked, "Are you all Christians? How did that happen?"

I shared with her my story and how God had visited me and my husband both on one night and how he had changed our lives so much. This is how we began talking about Christ and how powerful the true Word of God had been in our lives. I told her everything that had happened up until that point, and explained that we have complete faith that God has control of our lives and that we no longer even fear deportation or death back in Iran. I thank God that for some reason my testimony was very powerful to her and seemed to resonate in her heart right away. She was very excited and had lots and lots of questions just like I had had when I first started my journey to getting to know Christ. She then asked me how she could get a bible. Our home church had provided us with some Persian bibles and I gave her one right away, and recommended to her before she start reading to pray first and ask God to speak to her through His word. I also told her that if she had any questions at all, that she was more than welcome to ask me, or to join us once a month at our house for our Iranian Bible study.

Many Muslims are looking for concrete proof when they begin to learn about Christianity. She, however didn't ask for this sort proof. She mostly just listened in the beginning. I knew that she loved her son more than anything and I talked about God loves children and that we are all children in his eyes. As time went on though she became very curious and wanted to ask all sorts of questions. In fact, after a while it seemed to me that she would not accept anything without proof so I told her that she should consider coming to Bible study so she can learn about these subjects on a deeper level.

She was a single mom and was very private. It was obvious that she kept her personal life to herself, and was very hesitant to let anyone in. It was almost as if she had built a bubble around her and her son. I knew my next step would be to get Parvin out of her shell and open a little so she could meet people and make meaningful relationships at church like we had. So, I talked to Ida and asked if she could help find Parvin a small job that she could do that would get her out of the house. Ida recommended that she go to work for her aunt taking care of her because she needed a lot of help with all sorts of things due to her health. For example, she could take her to her doctor's appointments, or grocery shopping and other errands. Parvin was very excited when I told her the news and she couldn't wait to get started. I took her for the first time to meet her new employer, Mrs. Turus. I knew that up until that point Parvin had not made any Dutch friends at all, or Persian friends for that matter. I think our family was the first real relationship she had formed since coming to the Netherlands. I was so thankful that we were able to gain her confidence and introduce her to our wonderful church family. Soon after she started working for Mrs. Turus I could see a big change in Parvin. They got along so well and Mrs. Turus treated Parvin's son Sephr like a grandson. As her relationship grew with Mrs. Turus, Parvin's curiosity for the Bible also began to grow. In fact, not long after that Parvin was baptized into the Iranian church in Almere, and began holding her own Bible studies in her home. She worked for Mrs. Turus until she passed away just a couple of years ago, and Mrs. Turus left everything to Parvin and her son. I tell this story to illustrate the amazing things that God's love can do for people. We had never seen this sort of devotion to one another in our home country, and it was so touching to witness so many examples of how God's love can work through people as they love and care for one another.

Besides Parvin, there were also many other friends and people from the refugee center that became believers in Christ and their lives started to change dramatically as well. God has room for everyone in heaven but you must open your heart towards his son Jesus Christ and allow him to be the driver of your life. There are some people whose hearts are ready but because of how they were raised they have a lot of fear of Christianity. I can say with confidence that if we had never left Iran and had not encountered any of the problems that we went through, we could have been among those people that were still chained in the Islamic religion unable to see the truth.

We had learned in Islam that a girl from the age of 9 and a

boy from the age of 14 had to follow the Islam laws in every way. When I was just a girl of 9 years old, I had to pray 17 times a day without fail. If you multiply that by 365 days it comes out to a total of 6025 times a year I was praying in Arabic, a language which I could not understand. I was also expected to fast for 30 days a year during the month of Ramadan. From sunrise to sunset and we could not have a sip of water or any food. When I look back at it, the physical part wasn't the biggest problem. It was that I was being forced to do it without any understanding about why. I wasn't allowed to question anything to do with Islam, and as a female I was expected to keep my mouth shut on all things religious. I was also forced to wear the hijab from the age of 9. This is the headscarf that women wear in Islam that is meant to hide their hair so they don't temp men with their physical looks. According to the rules of Islam, if a man catches a glimpse of a woman's uncovered hair, the woman not the man mind you, will be hung upside down by their hair on the final day of judgement and cast into hell. For someone like me who did have a natural curiosity about how and why things were the way they were, it was very hard to exist without fear. I feared the wrath of Allah all the time and I was taught that the justice of God was very harsh and cruel for those that broke the rules.

The Koran was not the only source of rules either. Every time a new mullah would come into power new Sharia law books would be published that would lay out the new laws based on that leader's interpretation. Therefore, things in Iran continued to get worse and worse. When the Islamic revolution happened, it linked the religion as well as the mullah's interpretation and rules to the government, which meant that the court system was also tied to these things. Essentially it made it possible for the government or people in the government to use fear to control the people. How could anyone argue against rules and laws laid out through our religious teachings?

Another rule that was popularized during the time of the revolution was that of 'Jihad'. It literally means war in the name of

Allah against non-Muslims. All Jihadists were holy and be guaranteed a spot in heaven. You can imagine in such a culture of fear it was easy to use promises of paradise to lure devout Muslims into holy wars. After moving to the Netherlands, I learned even more about the Islamic religion and more about Muhammed himself. He himself waged holy wars. He used these wars to wield power and influence over people through violence and barbaric practices like torture and beheading. It was all in the name of Allah and to bring power to Muhammed. This was so directly the opposite of what Jesus taught that it was very hard for me to believe that people would willingly follow a religious teacher that promoted violence. Like Muhammed in these wars, the Koran then says that it is the Muslims' responsibility to cleanse the world of everything and everyone that is unclean so Islam can exist in a pure form touching every corner of the world. But I learned as a Christian the truth. God does not need any blood spilled to bless us. He needs our undying love, and faith, and to spread that to all people throughout the Earth.

After Muhammed, the Islamic religion believes in an additional 13 prophets that also all waged holy wars and promoted violence. One of Muhammed's grandsons was named Houssein, and he is considered one of the original prophets of Islam. He is the one that waged war against the Persian Empire that was headed by the famous Kings Kourosh and Syrus. By a stroke of luck, he was able to overtake the Persian army in an intense sandstorm. After his victory, he used violence to force the Islamic religion on the Persian people (modern day Iran) by killing all of their men and enslaving their women into marriage so they could reproduce and make children that would be raised Muslim. In the bloody attack against Persia, the Arabic forces had no mercy on women and girls. They took them as slaves or worse, and all ancient libraries full or irreplaceable texts were set on fire. They burned the libraries for days and days until all the books were gone. They also killed scientists and mathematicians to stamp out the long academic traditions of Persia. That savagery lingered like a blemish on the face of the Arabic history and in the memory of the Iranians. Even now Iranians are suffering from that imposed religion. History has it that at the time of the Arab's attack against Persia a tremendous tornado ripped through the frontier land so as the Persian soldiers came through they couldn't see the enemy. At long last Persia conceded that abject defeat. Otherwise the Arabic invaders would not have been strong enough to launch a war against Persia.

King Kourosh was very progressive, and before Houssein invaded Iran the country had made major advancements compared to other civilizations of that time. King Kourosh even created a declaration of human rights that was as all-encompassing and generous as any of the modern versions we have today. Looking back now I see that it would make sense that someone like me that had been brought up in such a fearful religion would naturally fear Christianity and try to avoid it to not be punished by Allah.

Sometimes I would encounter people like this in college or among my own friends, and I would remember all the things I went through. I was excited for them to also find the possibilities that come when you open your heart to God's love and the truth of His word. I wanted to spread God's love to everyone that I loved and to all the people from my country so they wouldn't have to go through the hardships that I went through. I knew that this was a calling on my life.

I learned though that what God wants is much higher and deeper than any of my thoughts and plans. In the times when our situation wasn't certain and we had no news in regards to our case. We would just focus on spreading the word of God with every chance we got. We witnessed so many amazing outcomes for new believers, and at that same time I began to understand the term spiritual warfare. I always seemed to be in immense pain whenever we'd witness a breakthrough from someone we knew. I was suffering so much with my physical pain from my hip at that time, but I tried to keep myself busy and remember that there is always victory in Jesus Christ. All this pain only served to make me more dedicated to spreading the word. We also spent a lot of time praying for my healing, and I was amazed to feel that my pain was relieved after several of our sessions.

Our Dutch friends had not experienced much in the way of direct healing through prayer and they always told us that they believed that God had placed us in their path to learn more about this kind of intense faith in God. They would tell us in the little time that we had become believers, God had touched us so much that they knew that God was going to use us to spread His word far and wide. We were so thankful that we had met such amazing, faithful people and that God had used our hardships to open our eyes to His truth.

During this time, I was still intensely learning more and more about the Bible, especially during Bible studies at our house and at Ida's home. We discussed everything at length and I was always so fascinated by the similarities to Islam, but also amazed at how different many of the stories were. One story in particular that stood out was the story of Isaac.

My whole life I had been taught in the Islamic religion that Ishmael was Abraham's chosen son, and every year in Iran they would celebrate the day that God asked Abraham to make Ishmael ready for sacrifice. God stopped this from happening though and instead placed a sheep on the sacrificial alter. Muslims call this day "Eyde Ghorban" which translates to the new sacrifice day, and whoever can travel to Mecca on that day sacrifices a sheep in honor of this story. Of course, it is told as the complete opposite in the Bible, and it explains that Isaac is in fact the chosen son. This variance between the two religions blew my mind. I knew that the Bible had been written before the Koran, and there was no way God could have made a mistake only to correct a story like that in the Koran. It was shocking to me. I began to realize that all our religious beliefs and traditions of Iran had been forced upon us by Arabic invaders, and did not come from any of our own history at all. I was beginning to question everything that I had ever known, even on a cultural level.

Some of the most atrocious rules and regulations in Islam came to my mind all the time as I tried to reconcile my upbringing with the truth that I now knew. For instance, according to Islam, when a girl turns nine years old she is expected to practice Islam just as an adult. It is also at this time that she has officially reached sexual maturity and is permitted to marry. Of course, not every family would permit this, but according to Islam, she is able to marry after that age and her husband can be young or very old. This is a practice that even goes back to Muhammed himself, when he married a nine-year-old girl named Ayesha in order to make peace between several Arab tribes. She was just one of his many wives. In fact, his first wife was an older wealthy woman of Jewish decent whom he married to build a religion around him, and to borrow history from the Jewish tradition. However, if you are the prophet of Allah, wouldn't there be another way to create peace between your people? Where is the peace? Why would God need anyone to marry and to possess a little girl in a sexual way to make peace between two nations? This is a part of the Islamic history. I don't have to make these questions up, they are there.

In truth, I now knew that our leaders had rationalized the unquenchable sexual desires of Arabic men by wrapping it up in a religious cover. I'm wondered how a God that could create the entire universe within six days was not able to invent a better way to sustain peace between his people. Once I learned the truth I truly grieved for my people and our culture. To realize how much was lost to this violent religion that was not even ours. To have been one of the greatest, most progressive ancient cultures of the world only to fall in this way.

Now even 1400 years after Muhammed and his family forced this religion on the Persian people, the effects are still rippling through our society. In the name of Islam, a man is still allowed to take a young child as his wife, and essentially rape this young woman at his will. We also still live with the rule that anyone who converts to another religion deserves to die, and if Jesus hadn't saved us on the night of December 4th 1995, we would have been deported to Iran and had been killed under this law. Thank God for the infinite treasure I found in my life, Jesus. When I first arrived in the Netherlands my only goal in life was to get my citizenship in that country, but that was no longer my heart's desire. I had a new purpose for living in Christ. I had truly found refuge in my salvation.

Today I hear that the Islamic regime still arrests Christians that take part in underground religious services. I thank God that I am saved by Christ from all that darkness and today I can share that light and treasure with other people no matter what physical hardships may come our way.

In the meantime, we received a letter from our lawyers to let us know about our case. None of it was very good news about our citizenship in the country. On the other side, I also received news from Iran in regards to the health of my mother. That was also a big burden on my shoulders, always worrying about her well-being. I would pray for her all the time and I tried calling her a few times a week even with all the problems we were going through my mom was always on my mind. Even when we lived with Mrs. Fiet I found a way to sneak out and make calls to my mother whenever I could. I knew that she needed to hear my voice just to know I was there thinking of her. It was right around this time that my father also slipped and fell and broke his hip. This meant that the only person that had been taking care of my mother was now also impaired.

My mother was lying in one corner of the house with Cancer and my dad was lying in another corner of the hospital with a broken hip. I felt so helpless being so far away. Because of his age he was also going through a lot of problems with his surgery, so in just a few days he had multiple surgeries. My mom didn't know about my dad's accident because my siblings decided it would be better for her not to know. She usually just waited, hoping that she'd soon be well enough to come visit us. And hoping to get better soon so she could come and visit me. It was about 5 years that I had been away from my mother at that point, and the only thing that connected us together were the telephone lines.

I called my mother much more after my father was hurt, though I never talked to her about Christ. It bothered me that I could not share this monumental change I had experienced in my life with my mother whom I loved so much. I wanted her to have the joy that Christ brings in her heart as well, but I was so nervous to bring it up because I knew she was still stuck behind the Islamic regime. I was reminded of the night I became a Christian myself. I would never forget that night when I told our Dutch pastor that I wanted to proudly bring the truth of Jesus to my country. I told him that I didn't want to be a lamp under the table, but rather, I wanted everyone to see the light that shines from me through Christ. By the time my mother was sick, I had already witnessed to many Iranian people, but I still didn't have the guts to witness to my own family. I had also kept my faith a secret from them up until that point.

One day my mom was feeling very badly and she asked my sister to call us so she could hear my voice, and say her goodbyes. When I heard her voice, it was very weak and I got very scared. I told her that she was always a very strong woman and that she must try to fight this. We talked for a little bit, and then she asked to speak to MJ. When MJ heard his Grandma's voice he also became very sad because he could hear how weak she was. She told him that it may be the last time he is able to speak to her before she was gone.

MJ immediately, without hesitation began telling my mother, "Grandma, where is your faith? If you just pray in the name of Jesus for your healing God is going to take care of you!"

I was in shock and didn't know what to do. I had been so scared to tell my mother about our conversion to Christianity and here was my child just blurting it out without any concern at all!

He continued, "I have read in the Bible that Jesus healed so many people and even rose someone from the dead. Grandma you must have faith and pray to God can heal you too."

As he was speaking I literally almost passed out from shock. I was thinking to myself that if my mom beats cancer, she will still die of a heart attack for sure after everything that MJ has told her! I couldn't say a word and my knees were numb. After MJ was done I didn't even want to take the phone back from him, so I had him give the phone to Omid. Omid was like a little parakeet and began to repeat everything that MJ had just said. I truly didn't know what to do at that point and just had them say goodbye and hung up the phone.

My husband Amin was always very helpful during tough situations like this, so I waited to talk to him about it before calling her back. I told him that I wanted to tell my mother myself about our faith and fully prepare her for the news. I also told him that I was worried that the way the kids had told her could be detrimental to her health. What would happen if my father and my siblings find out about this? If something happened to my mother, they all will blame me for it. Amin listened and answered calmly, " Why are you so worried? What if it was God's will, and while you were busy worrying God used the kids to tell her about it?"

He went on, "More importantly, it might have been a good time for your mother to know the truth so she can become a believer before she passes away."

Amin's words touched me and from that day on I started to pray for their health and salvation even more. A few days had passed since that day and one morning my mother called to talk to me. When I heard her voice, she sounded very healthy and she told me, “Sara I don't know what kind of prayer MJ said for me in the name of the Prophet Jesus, but I have to say that I feel a lot better today!"

When my mother said, she was feeling better right away I started to immediately give thanks to God His amazing plan. I truly believe that he used the kids to evangelize to my mother, and the whole time that I was worried God had turned it into her healing. At the end of our conversation that day my mother told me that she believes in the prophet Jesus, but that I can't ever forget that I'm a Muslim. She warned me to not be fooled into becoming an Armenian. This was of course because we only knew of Christians that were Armenian or Assyrian, and thought that it was a cultural thing. You could only become Christian if you were from these places.

She also told me that I must repent so I don't burn in hell, and so that she could forgive me as well. I just chuckled. There was no room to argue with my mother, so I simply told her not to worry, and that I would write her a letter very soon to tell her what had happened to us over the past few years. I asked her, "Please don't judge me or think about anything until you get my letter. Then when you read my letter then you can judge me."

Thankfully with the trust my mother had in me she accepted my request very easily and gave me her blessings. After that day, she and I would still talk a few times a week, and always I would talk to her about love of God and his healing. She would tell me that every time she would talk to me she would get peace and ask me where I have learned to speak like that and without me upsetting her I would tell her it's from God's word which has given me and my family peace and she said without any questions whatever it is nice to hear it from you.

My dad was getting better slowly as well, and still served my mother with love inspire of all his pain. My mother had gone through her chemo by then and the doctors would always encourage her with a positive attitude and tell her to stay positive to speed up her healing.

It was 1997 and we had put five years behind us and our situation was still the same. That year the Iranian church had a conference and they had invited all the Iranian pastors from around Europe so they can attend that conference. Farshid was one of the leaders of the Conference and he contacted us and told us to join them at the conference for a week so you get fed spiritually and you rest your body a little bit. I told him it's kind of hard for us to come for a week because of the situation we are in and he told us not to worry about that he will talk to Cor about it and if it's necessary for you guys to go back anytime I will take you guys back myself. The Dutch church were happy for this opportunity for us to be away from everything for a week and right away they talked to Amin's boss and gave him a week off as well so we can attend that conference for 6 days.

It was an amazing experience for us to enter a place where everyone was Christian and on top of that being Persian. Before we got to the conference we felt that our spirit and body was extremely tired and it needed a rest and we were in the right place at the right time where there was lots of love happiness and worship. It was a different experience for us I had never seen under one roof so many Iranian Christians with so many different Iranian pastors. It was a very spiritual and friendly atmosphere. We would wake up very early and before we did anything we would have a morning session of prayer and worship and it was such a sweet experience. We were looking to hide from our problems but at the same time we were seeking new experience and it was very easy to gain new experience being among so many believers.

Every day we would have praying worship and teaching session. I also volunteered in the kitchen to help Farah the mother of the young pastor Farshid. She oversaw the hospitality tables and meals she was such a loving lady with lots of wisdom. One of those days in an afternoon when we were sitting down having coffee we were having discussions of experiences we had while being a believer and how we got blessed from it. One of the members that was there was talking about the power of prayer he said that there was a pastor from Germany by the name Aramayes he said that he was in a couples group and his wife could not get pregnant and the teaching that day was about the power of prayer after service him and his wife went to pastor Aramayes and asked him to pray so his wife could get pregnant. Pastor Aramayes asked them the Child that God is going to give to you guys do you want it to be a boy or a girl. That couple that wanted a child for many years said we don't care about the sex of the child if God blesses us with a child we are very thankful. Pastor Aramayes prayed for that couple and the year after God gave them a son.

I approached the pastor Aramayes and I asked him is it true that when you pray for the sex of the child God is going to give you that and he said absolutely he said if you pray with faith according to God's word you can even move mountains. I told him to be honest I have to Sons and I always wanted a girl and when I heard this testimony today I would like you to pray for me and my husband as well so God can bless us with a little girl. He said okay when we have our prayer meeting tonight come with your husband and we will pray in unity for you guys so God can bless you with a daughter. I was so excited that from that moment I could see myself having a daughter. After prayer that night we went to pastor Aramayes and asked him to pray for us. He asked my husband do you know why we are gathered here to pray and Amin told him "no" my wife just said let’s go to pastor Aramayes so he can pray for us. The pastor told him that your wife came to and asked me to pray for you guys so God can bless you 2 with a daughter. Right away Amin told him I do not want another child while we are going through all this stuff we have 2 sons already and I thank God for them and honestly that is enough for us specially in the situation we are in right now. Right there I looked at Amin and with a begging tone and look asked him well let him at least pray for us so when the day comes that we want a child it will be a girl. Amin with a firm tone said the 2 sons we have is enough I do not want another child we don't even know our future or our children future so I ask you not to bring this up or talk about this anymore.

I was very sad and ashamed in front of that pastor and I was very quiet and that pastor with love told us that you 2 need to come to an agreement for a child that we will pray for the sex of it. After that night, every opportunity I had I would beg Amin and tell him that I don't want a child now let's have him at least pray for us and we will also ask God for his timing for me to have another child. I was begging the whole time and Amin was denying the whole situation at all costs. The rest of the days of the conference was full of blessings and we experienced so much we got baptized in the Holy Spirit and speaking in tongues. We had to say our goodbyes now from all those people that we met at the conference and it was kind of hard because we had gotten so close with each other and it seemed like we have known each other for many years. After one week coming from the conference I felt like I have gained a new strength and I was full of energy and happiness and our Dutch friends saw those changes as well and they were very happy and they would tell us in all these years' you guys were here you should have gone on a little vacation because it is good for you guys to have a change of scenario.

That summer one of our friends Martin Plump who was a very friendly guy and they were going on vacation and it was kind of custom there if someone would go on a long-distance vacation they would let someone use their home as vacation home. That year Family plump asked us if wanted to stay at their house for a few days while they are on vacation and he said we could use everything in the house and its good for you guys to get away from your house for a while and for the kids. We accepted their offer with joy and happiness so they let us use their house and everything that was in it which was amazing because we were not the same race or family but they shared their home with us and the only thing that we were was brother and sisters in Christ. I thank God that his love is so amazing that he gets all the nations closer to each other and make them in one unity. When the time came and we went over and walked into the kitchen we saw a letter that was written by Martin Plump's wife and it was a letter with full of love and instructions saying that please feel comfortable while you guys are here and we have filled the fridge and the pantry room with food for you guys and it should be enough for one whole week and that they had provided us with all kinds of hygiene for each one of the bedrooms that we were staying in so we would feel comfortable. I had never seen that kind of love and especially in my own country and my eyes were full of tears and how God has put such an amazing Christians in our path that they even let us use their home. The few days we were there we were very happy and was resting a lot and the kids were enjoying it as well because it was such a big house and so different from our little apartment.

Every chance I would get I would also tell Amin how my dream is to have a little girl and he would not give up and always bring up our immigration stuff and how our sons got so hurt and why do you want to add another problem to our problems but I wouldn't listen and I would still have faith and hope. The school year had started again and my college also started and one of my classmates who were an Iranian/Armenian lady by the name of Juliet asked me about our immigration status. I told her No we are still waiting to get an answer. She asked me how many times you guys have been denied in these past few years that you are here in the Netherlands. I told her we have been denied 3 times but now we have a few good lawyers that are working on our case. Juliet told me why don't you guys Apply for the Unites States I work for the Un and over there are applying for Us after being denied once and now they are trying their best to get to US. You have a great case and you will for sure get your citizenship in the US. I would always know after going through all those hardships they were either going to give our citizenship there or they would deport us back to Iran and I never thought for another solution and I didn't want to think about it either because I could not change my future with force and I tried with respect to keep myself busy with other student in class and try to avoid continuing that conversation. Juliet would not give up on me and every time she saw me she was encouraging me to apply. Finally, one day I told her we became believers in this country and we found some amazing and great friends through that and we love them a lot and we don't like to leave them unless they force us to leave the country. It seemed like she was not accepting anything I was saying so she asked me to call her one time at work and ask them for the application for the Unites States and she told me trust me it is free and it has no cost all you must do is to take the first step and make a call and ask for an application and after that they will take care of the rest.

Finally, I told her okay you bring the forums and help me and I will fill it out she said that first we are not allowed and second it has to be your request either by telephone or show up there so they can give you the forums or mail them to you. I was ashamed of her asking me so much and tired of it as well so I talked to Amin about it and we concluded that we are going to call and request those forums. When we called, they asked us our name and identity and how long we have been living in the Netherlands and about our immigration status and how many times our case has been denied and we have been deported. I answered them in very short sentences and after our phone conversation they asked us for our address and told us you guys are pre-approved for a green card in the unites States and we will send you very soon all the forums please fill out and send it back to us so we can work on your case right away.

After 2 weeks, we received a package from the UN with all the forums which were in English there was also a letter in Dutch and English asking us all the documents we need additional to filling out the forums and send it to them. I took those forums and put them in a closet and I thought to myself okay I did what Juliet told me to do but there is no need in filling those forums but every time she saw me at school she would ask me did you feel the forum out yet hurry up and do it and send it in and my response to her was I will feel it out soon we have a lot of time don't worry. Finally one day that she asked me I told her honestly I can't fill it out and I don't want to apply for another country because we want to stay in the Netherlands and nowhere else we have a lot friends here that are closer to us then our own family and I don't want to think about going somewhere else, thank you that you are thinking of us so much and I am ashamed because every time you saw me you would ask me and I would give you lots of excuses and because of that I decided to be honest with you and talk to you.

Juliet looked at me and said to me with a very kind tone "sweetie when you apply doesn't mean you're going right away to US these paper works can take months and if you receive your citizenship here is good then you don't have to worry about it but if you don't without any money out of your own pocket you have another door open for you". She told me after all these years going through so much trouble and not knowing your living situation at least you know there is another country like Us which is everyone's dream to go there and you have their Green card in your hand and you can go to US without any cost, think about it God might have opened another door for your family after all the trouble you have gone through. After she told me all these things with so much love and humbleness it kind of was sitting right in my heart and that night when Amin came home I talked to him about it again and he agreed with me to fill the forums out. It took about a few weeks for us to fill the forums out with the help of someone that was working for the immigration office and we send them to the UN department without any hope or any inspiration to get a positive result to make us happy.

We received a letter from our lawyer saying that Amin had to start the process over again by going to a refugee center so they can open his case again with a higher judge. The lawyers in the meantime guaranteeing us that nothing would happen to

Amin but I was were worried and I could not be calm no matter what I was worried so bad that I would get dizzy and throw up. One day Amin went with one of our Dutch friends to a Refugee center close to a border and he started the process that we did few years ago over again but this time he was alone. He told me that he waiting for a long time in that like and when it was his turn it was closing time and they told everyone that was waiting in that like that they can serve them anymore that day and they must come back tomorrow.

That day I was dizzy the whole time and was feeling very sick and Rima who was living at our house told me lets go to the doctor or the Emergency room but I didn't want to go and one of the reasons was that I didn't want to leave the kids alone home while Amin was gone and the second reason I had I didn't have insurance and didn't want the church to pay for my hospital visit. That evening someone rang the doorbell and it was Amin and we were very surprised and happy to see him and we thought everything was done but Amin explained to us what had happened and I told him maybe it was God's will and he didn't want you to start this process alone.

I was feeling still very dizzy and I had no control while I was walking and Amin who didn't know what had happened he was very worried. That night when the Pastor of the church found out I wasn't feeling good he came over to our house to visit me and the first question he asked was why you didn't go to the doctors. I told him that I will waited till tomorrow to see how I feel and if I am not okay by then I will go to the doctors but Rima said she didn't go to the doctors because she doesn't have insurance. Pastor Blenk was very sad and said what is the church for then we must witness you like this and because you don't have insurance don't even think about it you must go to the hospital tonight and all the cost of the hospital the church will take care of it. While the pastor was still in the room Rima helped me to go to the restroom and while we were going to the restroom I got dizzy very bad and started to bleed a lot and I passed out. When I opened my eyes, I was in the emergency room and there was a medical team taking care of me. (They found chunks of blood it was so big that they thought she had a miscarriage. They took that big chunk of blood in to the laboratory to see what it is. In the meantime, my blood pressure was very low and they could not get my blood pressure to a normal level. I was dizzy for hours and I could notice my surrounding and it was so many people around me and the doctors were trying their best.) I could see everything but I had not movement in my body finally after hours they were successful of bringing my blood pressure to a normal level but because of a very bad headache I was screaming a lot till they finally gave me some morphine to make the pain go away.

My headache was still there but I had no energy to scream and I would only call the names of my kids and my husband. I don't know how many hours had passed away and because of all the medications they gave me I was a sleep a lot and when I opened my eyes I saw my husband besides me with tears in his eyes and he was holding my hand and was praying for me and his love and the way he looked at me would give me so much energy but again my eyes would fade away and I would pass out. Later, the doctors told me that I was awake and in a coma for about 36 hours still throughout those 36 hours I would sense Amin next to me the whole time and I would also fell the warm of his tears falling on my arms. After I was feeling a little bit better the doctors started to do some tests on me and everything seemed normal and even those chunks of bloods was not what they thought and they said the reason of all that bleeding was because of too much stress. Because I had lost a lot of blood they decided to collect some Cerebral Spinal fluid so they can test it and the cause of that were lots of stress and after 48 hours through my Spine they inserted blood into my body. I was at the hospital for about 7 days so they can do all kinds of tests on me and they said because you are young your body fought it very well in other cases people can stay in coma for days or maybe months. Even though the doctors didn't know anything about our life and what kind of issues and problems we have gone through these past few years they recommended to us that I can't be in any kind of environment that causes me to have stress.

At the time, I was at the hospital our friends and pastor did not leave us alone even after I was released home they tried to visit me every single day and taking care of me and the kids. It was a very hard time for us and just the look on Amin's face it seemed like he has ages so much but he was taking care of me with so much love and kindness that it seemed like I was just born. The love of my husband and God always gave me and un-explainable strength and I always wanted to do whatever is in my power for God because he has loved me so much and for my husband who has been by my side through everything in all our problems our happiness and has cried by my side with all my pains that I have gone through all these years and I always want to pour out my love at his feet. Sometimes I would think to myself how blessed I am that God has put Amin in my life because we were a whole every time we were together. Besides our first year of marriage because we were still getting to know each other everything was beyond good. The reason I am saying the first year is because when we got engaged and married we only knew each other for 1 month and we had no time to get to know each other on a personal level, but today we are very happy of the choice we made in each other and we thank God that he put us together.

CHAPTER 20

My recovery was well on underway and after I had been home for a bit, Pastor Blenk came over to visit. He asked me if I had gotten the bill from the hospital yet, but I had not. I was a little concerned that the bill would be very high especially considering I had been taken for procedure twice while I was there. I asked Pastor Blenk how much he thought the total bill might be. He smiled and told me not to worry about it. He said that whether it was one Guilden or ten thousand it didn't matter and the church was prepared to pay it of us.

"We know that God is going to bless it because we are using it to help one of His children in need. We are putting it in his hands," he said.

By the time four months had passed we still hadn't received a bill from the hospital for my stay and surgery. The accounting department from the church diligently contacted us every week asking if we had heard from them, but each week the answer was the same. We hadn't heard a word.

The church then began trying to get in contact with the billing department at the hospital directly, and find out how much we owed. To their surprise the hospital told them that they had no record of anyone by my name receiving any care there. They said that there was no record of my registration, and no record of any services at all. Therefore, there was no cost and no bill had ever been created.

The members of the church were shocked by this news and didn't know exactly what to make of it. Amin and I were not surprised though. We had witnessed first-hand how God had taken care of us from the very beginning, and ever since our salvation, the church members were witnessing it too. Before we came along that church had been very traditional, but now they were all witnessing the power of God in a new and exciting way. They saw how God works miracles even today for those that are faithful to Him, and it was cause for much excitement and new enthusiasm in the church.

Things settled down a bit after that and we waited for word on our immigration case. A few weeks later we finally received word from our lawyer. He said that the government wanted both of us to start the entire process over again. This meant that we'd both have to go back to a refugee camp to work through the paperwork properly. He also assured us that it wouldn't take long this time around, and that the administrators were all very aware of our situation and that they'd make sure the decision was quick. I was totally against this idea. After all those years, there was no way I could bring myself to start over again. I was just fully recovering and was busy praying to God to finally bring me that baby girl I so desperately wanted, and the last thing I wanted was to go back to the beginning. I wanted to stay where we were and feel settled.

Pastor Blenk found out that they wanted us to start our refugee application process over again, and he wrote a letter to the representative of the Protestant Party to tell him about our situation. He also sent a petition in support of us along with his letter that had been signed by thousands of Christian families all throughout Holland. This representative response almost immediately to Pastor Blenk and knew our case very well because of the previous media coverage. He agreed to have a meeting and invited us all to an event where we could also meet someone high up in the Dutch government named Mrs. Smith (the Dutch Foreign Minister). This way we'd also be able to hopefully bring her attention to our situation as well.

The event also included dinner, and the plan was for us to meet with Mrs. Smith during dinnertime and explain our case to her then. Pastor Blenk and I went together to the event in Den Haag. When we arrived, we were taken right away to our designated seats for the speech, and then afterward were escorted to a beautiful room where dinner was to be served. I was touched by how respectful everyone was. I was still a refugee to them, yet they never acted as if I was any different than they were. By that time, I had earned my diploma from the local college and could speak Dutch very well. I could see that they were surprised by this, and many asked me how I found time to learn the language with all the hardships we had gone through. I explained to them that it was an honor for me to be in their country and I wanted nothing more than to simply become a Dutch citizen. Our family wanted that with all our hearts.

After dinner, we were told that Mrs. Smith was coming over to speak to us in regards to our immigration case. They also asked me to personally say a few words to her, and not to worry or to be nervous about it. Of course, I was still very nervous about the whole thing. I didn't know exactly how to speak to her or what I should say. I was lost in my own thoughts when a nicely dressed lady came over to our table with another gentleman. She had a very serious look on her face and I could see that she was very distinguished. Pastor Blenk and I stood up when they came to our table and respectfully introduced ourselves to them.

With much love and kindness, she told us that she was very sorry for all the problems that we'd had to go through over the past few years, and that she had involved herself personally in our case. She went on to explain that she didn't understand why the judge kept denying our case, and assured us that she was going to do everything she could to help get our case approved as soon as possible. Pastor Blenk and I thanked her so much for her time and her concern before she left the table and moved on to the other many issues she was discussing that night. That evening was unforgettable. I couldn't believe that someone who was so far up in the Dutch government had taken her time to come and meet a person like myself. She had been so kind and obviously concerned for our welfare. I thought about how something like this would never have happened in Iran, and I hoped that someday that would change.

About two weeks after the event we received a letter from our lawyer again. This time it stated that we had to report to a refugee center to restart our immigration case. We were very confused by this letter after the conversation we had with Mrs. Smith. Why did we have to report to a refugee center again? After all the special attention, and the phone calls to lawyers and media attention, how could this happen again? We called the lawyer's office and found out that it was true, and that the judge made his final decision. Amin and I would have to report to another refugee center so we could restart our case. Fortunately, they told us that we would only be there for about a week to complete the process, and it was not necessary for the kids to come with us. We were hopeful that this was going to be a solution, but after all our problems it was hard to believe that it would be that easy, or that we'd only be there for a week. For some reason, something always seemed to go wrong, and we were worried that this would be another time where that held true.

I remember the morning we were supposed to leave; Ida came to pick the kids up for school and MJ was acting very badly toward all of us. He was angry that Amin and I had to go back to the refugee center and was taking it out on everyone. I tried to explain to him that this was a far better alternative to being deported back to Iran, but it was hard for him to fully understand and accept that. We told him that everything was going to be ok, and that all he had to do was lean on God and pray for us whenever he was worried.

He left with Ida and had tears in his eyes and you could see that he was sick with anxiety. Mrs. Fiet's husband then picked us up shortly after and drove us all the way to the refugee center we were supposed to report to. It was nearly two and a half hours away. Most of the way there we sat in silence. We could tell that Mrs. Fiet's husband was worried about us as well, but he was so loving and supportive and he tried to keep things positive. I was calm most of the way and wasn't worried at all until we took a turn down a dense forest road. It was unlike anywhere else we had ever been before and I began asking Mrs. Fiet's husband if he knew any details about this camp, and why it was so far out in the wilderness.

He told us that he had heard that this refugee camp was in an old prison camp built by the Nazis during World War II. All the other camps were filled at that time, and this was the only place that had space for us. We finally arrived at this building or should I say a prison? It had very long concrete walls and right in front of the entrance there were guards on either side armed with guns. This was a sight that I was not accustomed to seeing in the Netherlands and as soon as I saw them my stomach began to turn with nervous energy.

Mrs. Fiet's husband hugged me and then said a prayer with us before heading back to his car. He said a few kinds encouraging words and then drove away. We were alone there. It felt like we were back at the start of our journey all over again. We began walking toward the entrance and spoke to the first two guards there. We gave one of them our paperwork that the lawyers had given us, and he escorted us inside to a small waiting room. He told us to wait there until another guard came to take us to another building. While we were waiting, I tried to look outside, but couldn't see much because the building was like a fortress, surrounded with cold concrete walls. Amin and I were praying while we waited, and I could feel my hands getting colder and colder until I was shivering. Finally, the other guard came in and politely introduced himself before walking us to the next building.

I must say that even though the place was cold and scary, the people, were just as warm and welcoming as all the other Dutch people we had met along the way. It was comforting to know that we were surrounded by kind people who cared for us.

As we were walking to the other building I saw all sort of

people just leaning against the walls and you could see that all of them were very welcoming. We then found ourselves waiting inside another room before they were supposed to call us in for our intake interview. I was not feeling too well by that point and I asked the guard if I could use the restroom. My stomach was feeling off and it seemed like my nerves had gotten the better of me. I literally felt like I was about to throw up. My blood pressure also felt very low.

The guard followed me to the restroom to make sure that I was okay. After a few minutes, had passed, he began calling my name and asking me to get out of the bathroom. I was afraid and didn't know what to do. I was throwing up and couldn't just walk out, but I was also so worried about upsetting the guard. Finally, they called in a female guard to come and check on me. She came and could see immediately that I wasn't well, so they called a paramedic to come and take me to the medical office on a stretcher.

I was in the medical office for a while so the doctor could do a full examination on me. After a he completed a few tests he came back into the room with his chart and asked me, "Do you know how many months along you are?"

At first I didn't understand his question and was totally confused. I asked him to repeat his question, and he said, "How many months pregnant are you?"

I must have still had the confused look on my face because the doctor then said, "You are pregnant, and everything looks fine but your blood pressure is very low. So, you'll have to rest a bit and see if this IV drip will help level things out."

I was in complete shock. I had not expected this news at all. I was also so full of excitement that I had to tell Amin the good news right away. I told the doctor that I couldn't possibly stay in bed after receiving this news! He told me to lie back down and that he would get Amin for me.

Amin came into the room and I immediately blurted out, "I'm pregnant!"

He didn't know what to think at first. I could see he was also in shock, but that shock quickly turned to excitement. Both of us were so focused on this amazing good news and all our anxiety about being back in a camp went away completely. We almost forgot all about it! All I could think about was how God had finally decided to bless me with a daughter. I don't know why I was so convinced in my spirit that this new baby would be a girl, but I was. I was convinced that God had heard my prayers and blessed us once again.

A few moments later one of the guards came into the medical office and asked about my health status. The doctor checked my vital signs again and said that my blood pressure had improved but not enough for me to be up out of bed. He gave the guard a note and told him that he would let them know when I'd be able to move around again. I still had a strange pain in my stomach and I asked the doctor what he thought it might be. I was concerned that maybe I was having a miscarriage. The doctor told me that my blood pressure dropping could have put a lot of stress on the baby and that is why we must keep you in bed and monitor your vital signs until we know for sure that everything is okay. In that moment, I immediately began to pray for my baby and for peace for myself and my husband. The doctor then gave me a shot that calmed me down a little and I fell asleep for a while. When I opened my eyes, it was already 4pm and Amin was sitting very calmly next to me. I wasn't feeling any pain anymore, and I tried to get off the bed slowly. The nurse stopped me and told me to wait for the doctor's approval before I moved around.

The doctor came in and checked me over. He then told us that he had spoken to the people in charge of the center, and because of my health situation they agreed to complete all our paperwork that day so we could go home that night! The only problem was that the person who dropped us off would have to come back to pick us up that same day. They didn't have a full medical center and were concerned that if anything happened to me or the baby, they would not be able to help us. Amin told me that some of the people he had spoken to in the waiting room had been there for weeks waiting to complete the intake process. There was one big main living area that had been divided into two sections. One area was for single people and the other was for families. While we were there they served everyone a simple meal that consisted of two pieces of bread with cheese and a slice of meet. They also were given a small carton of milk. It seemed like that refugee center was like a prison designed to break the will of the people there. Maybe if the process was frustrating enough they would just give up and decide to go back to their countries. When we had arrived there I had noticed how all the employees were just standing around drinking coffee, chit chatting with each other. I wondered if they knew what kind of hardship we were all feeling. Just waiting to know what our futures looked like. Even though we were now going to be able to dramatically shorten the time we'd have to spend there, we still felt horribly for the people still stuck inside.

I did my interview in the nurse's office and the whole process was very short. Amin did his in another room and after they took our fingerprints and pictures for new identification cards, they told us that we were eligible for all the benefits of a refugee. They asked us if there is someone picking us up and Amin told them yes, that he had called Ida's husband and he might have already arrived. They called the guard at the gate and sure enough, he said that there was a car there waiting for us. In the meantime, they were scrambling to do all our paperwork very fast so they could dismiss us as soon as possible.

When we were saying goodbye to the immigration officer told us that we were very lucky to have been interviewed so fast, and to remember that when your child is born to thank them for bringing you good luck even while still in the womb. He quickly got me a wheelchair and proceeded to escort us out to the entrance of the camp. As we made our way through, we saw so many eyes on us. All the poor people stuck in that place were looking at us with slight jealousy, but also just wondering why we could leave so quickly. My heart broke for them and I began to pray and ask God to help ease their suffering and to make their immigration process move quickly. I was so excited to get home and tell MJ and Omid our amazing news, but it was also so heart wrenching to leave all those people there without any answers for them.

Finally, we exited the building and began walking towards the dark driveway. It was pitch black and the only place that was lit was the guardhouse a few hundred yards away. We saw a man standing between the guardhouse and the wall trying to keep himself warm because the wind was so strong that night. The wind in the Netherlands can get unbelievably strong at times, and that night was very bad.

As we got closer to him we noticed that he was a black man, and assumed he must have been Somalian or North African. Amin and I walked towards the man and Amin asked him what he was doing there at that time of night. He explained to us that he came there to register as a refugee for the second time. He stood in line for hours and when it came to his turn the office had closed. It was already dark by then and there was no car for him to take him to a hotel or anything. He said he was afraid of getting lost in the woods so he assumed the safest place to be was right there in front of the guard house. That way he'd be first in line when they opened in the morning. I couldn't believe how they had left this poor man to stand out in the cold all night! I realized how sometimes rules and regulations don't make sense in the real world, and often they prevent human beings from being open and loving with each other. Would it have been a huge inconvenience to bring this man inside for the night? Of course, not, but because it was against the rules it could not be done.

We asked him if he had eaten anything that day and he

told us that he did get a sandwich during the lunch hour but that was it. We had brought some snacks with us from home and we hadn't eaten them so we gave him the food so he would have something to sustain him until the morning. We then said goodbye and walked towards the car that was waiting for us. Ida's husband Frans had come to pick us up and when he saw us approaching he jumped out of the car and hugged us very tightly. When we got into the warm car we realized how cold it was outside, and after we the car had been moving for less than 30 seconds, Amin asked Frans to stop the car. He ran out and gave his jacket to the man waiting by the guard station. He hugged Amin very hard and thanked him for his kindness. Then he asked Amin to pray for him. Frans and I were watching Amin and the man outside the car with tears rolling down our faces. It was a beautiful moment for all of us.

Amin got back into the car and Frans told him that he had a very kind heart, "Even though you are going through problems and hardships you still pay attention to other people and help them whenever you can."

That night we got home around midnight and when we opened the door MJ and Omid jumped into our arms. We thought that they'd be staying at Ida's house but Ida said that MJ begged her to bring them back to wait for us when he heard we were coming home. Everyone was so happy that we had forgotten about time. We also remembered that there were so many people from the church that were probably up praying for us, so we decided to give them all a call before going to bed just to let them know we were home safe. The next day we went to the social services office and introduced ourselves with our new id cards. Then, just like they had on our first day in the country, us insurance and our salary. I was feeling very good that day. I was consumed with dreams of our future, and of our baby that would be coming. I was so thankful that we did not have to stay at that refugee center for more than a day. I knew for sure that none of this was because of any man's will, but because it was God's will. I had prayed for His favor and blessings over us and he had turned a situation that could have dragged out into months into only a few hours.

When we got to church that Sunday, everyone was extremely happy to see us. They were all showering us with love and attention. Some of the men were even holding out their jackets for Amin to take after Frans had told them the story of the man freezing outside of the refugee center. He was embarrassed by all the attention and told them that he had only done what God's Word tells us to do. He had a couple of jackets at home and God's Word says that when you have two of something, you should give one of them to a brother or sister in need.

Everyone was also very excited to hear about my pregnancy. They were all congratulating me talking about what a blessing this new baby was going to be. In many ways, I felt like we had avoided a horrible situation and were back to living our normal lives there in Delft among our friends and church family. Besides a little morning sickness, the next few months were relatively uneventful as we waited for the next step in the immigration process. I even brought MJ and Omid to one of my doctors' appointments where they saw the baby on the sonogram. They begged me to find out the sex of the baby, but I stayed strong. I wanted to wait until the baby was born for the big surprise. It was a lovely, peaceful time for a bit.

Even my mother seemed to be feeling better during that time. We would have long conversations nearly every week, and she seemed more hopeful than she had been. She was so excited about my new pregnancy as well. I encouraged her to stay positive and with God's help we'd soon have our living situation finalized. The church also decided to try and surprise me by sponsoring a visit to the Netherlands for my mother. They arranged all the documents and brought them to me to sign. It was such a wonderful gesture and I was so thankful.

I had been in a lot of pain toward the end of my

pregnancy, mostly because of my hip and the pressure the pregnancy had put on it. My daily level of pain was getting worse and worse from my hip, but I tried to push it out of my mind as much as possible. Besides, when it came to the extra pain from the pregnancy, I didn't let it bother me because I knew that it was all for a good reason. I just couldn't wait to hold my new baby, and I knew that would be enough to never think of the pain again.

Finally, the day arrived. September 16, 1998 was the day that the doctor had scheduled for my C-section. He felt that with all my health problems that this was the safest way to ensure that the baby and myself would be okay. Amin and I were so full of hope and excitement as we left for the hospital. I took the pink dress I had purchased when I first found out I was pregnant, and Amin had decorated the house to welcome the baby home. We got to the hospital and were immediately prepped for surgery. I was so thankful because Amin could be there with me the whole time. In Iran, the men are not allowed to be present at the births of the children, so this was a very special experience for us to share.

A short time after the procedure started, the doctor finally held the baby up and said, "You have a beautiful baby girl!"

Tears of joy were streaming down Amin's face and we were both crying together thanking God. We had been blessed again with this little life, and we had finally gotten our baby girl! Our level of thankfulness was truly beyond words. I was in an immense amount of pain after the surgery and they had given me Morphine to help with it, but I still remember everything from that day. It was one of the most beautiful days of my life and it will stay with me always.

The dream I always had of having a little girl was finally a reality and after discussing it with Amin and the boys we named her Roya. The name Roya means "beautiful dream". Because of my health and possible complications, I had to stay at the hospital for 7 days. Lucky for me I had a lot of visitors to keep me company! I can safely say that I had visitors from over 70 families that came everyday with love to see me and bring me bouquets of flowers. I was never alone or feeling lonely, they took great care of me every step of the way. Today now that I am writing this and thinking about that day, I still have the same overwhelming feeling of gratitude to God. It was such a wonderful answer to so many of my prayers.

When Amin came to pick us up from the hospital I could see that he was very excited to finally can bring Roya and me home. The moment we arrived at the apartment I saw that he had placed flowers on the floor all the way through to the entrance. He had decorated the house so beautifully and had soft peaceful music playing with the lights perfectly dimmed. I was overwhelmed by all of it, and I couldn't believe how lucky I was to be married to an amazing man like Amin. Everything that we had gone through together was all worth it, and our family was finally complete. I felt truly loved and special.

When the boys got home from school they couldn't sit still with excitement, and it seemed like that little angel had already brought so much joy to our home. They took turns holding Roya, and even Amin waited his turn to hold his little girl. I could see that he was beyond happy. We had lots of visitors for a few days that all wanted to come see Roya and me. They came from all over, from cities that we used to live in to Delft and they brought so many gifts for the baby. At that same time my mom's visa was being processed for her to come to visit us. The last few times I had talked to her, her voice seemed very tired and it seemed like she was in a lot of pain. She was trying to hide it from me but I could tell she wasn't doing well. I tried to encourage her and tell her that if we were lucky she may even be able to make the baby shower. In Holland baby showers are given after the baby is born, and I'd always tell her this to keep her faith alive, but I could tell that things were getting hard for her.

Roya was about two months old when my mom's health

turned very bad. She had an appointment to go to the Dutch Embassy for an interview before she could get approval to leave the country, but because of her chemo therapy she missed the appointment. We knew then that things must be very bad. The doctors told my family that they didn't think she'd be alive for much longer, and that all they could do at that point was to ease her pain by giving her lots of Morphine. I talked to her twice a day until slowly she wasn't able to talk anymore. They would put the phone next to her ear so she could at least keep hearing my voice. My voice that was coming from another continent over a small wire. I felt so helpless that this was all I could do for her in her last days. Inside of me I was screaming and missing my mother so much, but I tried to hold back my emotions over the phone to try and keep her spirits up. Even after all of that I held out hope that God would give us a miracle and heal her so she could come to the Netherlands.

That final sickness lasted a few more weeks until December 18th, 1998. That day when I called the house it seemed to be very noisy in the background. My brother began talking and I realized that my mother had passed away. A part of my joy was taken away from me that day. Just knowing that I couldn't at least hear her breathe through the telephone line one more time broke my heart and made me feel lost in many ways. I wanted to scream as much as I could just to empty my heart of sadness. I cried and I cried at the thought that I could never hold her or see my mother again. Separation from the ones we lover are so bitter especially when it comes to death. I wished I could hold her once more just to place my head for a moment on her chest and feel that love of a mother that is irreplaceable. I put Roya's head on my chest and cried uncontrollably for some time. After that night Roya, would not drink my milk anymore because it began to taste bitter and finally dried up because of all my sadness and stress. A day or so later I was still distraught and had come down with a fever. Amin rushed me to the doctors and was worried because he hadn't seen me this way in quite a long time.

We returned from the doctors a few hours later, and Amin went to the mailbox before helping me into the house. He was holding the mail in his hands reading through it when I said jokingly, "Why are you in such a hurry to get the mail and leave me standing by the front door like this? It's not like we are having any good news coming our way!"

Amin looked up at me and smiled and said, "Who knows? Maybe this time we will get good news!"

I laughed and told him, "Oh sure! Maybe we'll get some good news from the President of the United States himself!"

We came into the apartment and Amin was laughing very hard. He and said, "Sara you were right, we did receive an important letter from the United States. From the American embassy, actually."

I told him that he must be kidding, but he assured me that it was true. He told me to come over and see it for myself. He was right! We had received a letter from the UN by way of the American embassy. However, instead of good news, inside was a notice that our case for seeking asylum in the United States had been denied due to lack of proper paperwork. I knew that this had been a possibility because I hadn't been able to find a few of the items they had asked for. It was disappointing but it didn't worry us that much because we were still so focused on getting citizenship in the Netherlands. With everything going on with the loss of my mother and having a new baby at home, we were just thankful that we had not heard any bad news from the Dutch government. We hadn't heard any news at all, but at least we had not heard a bad decision yet. We just wanted to stay positive and faithful until something happened. Our lawyers told us around that time that our case was the most complicated and frustrating case they'd ever worked on.

CHAPTER 21

It was nearly a month after my mother passed away that we had Roya baptized in the church. Agate, Ellen's mother from Krimpen became her Godmother. We had managed to stay close with them after all those years even though it was about an hour and half away from our home in Delft. It was a huge honor to have such a wonderful woman be committed to helping us raise our precious new daughter in the Christian faith. It was also right around this time that we finally did hear from another Dutch judge that had been given our immigration case. To our shock and surprise it was another denial letter. It was shocking to me that after all the trouble we had been through, and even getting to meet Mrs. Smith who is at the highest levels of Dutch government, we still could not get a positive result. It was truly baffling.

By that time, we had gotten used to receiving bad news, and every time something seemed overwhelming we'd simply lean on our faith in God and trust that He would provide for us. We truly gave all our worries and our concerns over to God. We laid them all at the foot of the cross and lived in our faith that He would take care of us and provide for us per His will. So, we kept hope alive for another round of appeals. Then one day we received a very unexpected letter from the U.N. We assumed that it was another form letter related to our denial of our case much like the one we had already received before. However, this letter was not like the first one. This letter started off with, "Congratulations! You will be going to Frankfurt, Germany very soon to complete an interview and to turn in your additional paperwork."

I was confused and didn't know what to make of it. Which one of the letters was correct? I was certain that the second one had to be a mistake or a clerical error. After all, we had not turned in the proper paperwork so I thought there was certainly no way we'd be granted asylum there. I called the U.N. Office in Den Haag right away and spoke to a lady there on the phone. I explained that we had received two letters that appeared to be completely the opposite of one another. She asked me to read each letter aloud to her and then put me on hold to investigate further. When she returned, she told me that in fact the second letter was correct! She told me that we had been approved to go to the United States and that we'd be receiving information very soon on when we were supposed to go for our interview in Germany. I was speechless.

I fumbled over my words and managed to tell the woman "thank-you" before I hung up the phone. When I Amin got home I immediately explained what had happened, and waited the outburst of excitement I expected from him. That is not what happened at all though. Amin was totally opposed to accepting this invitation to go to Frankfurt for a further interview and was worried that it might jeopardize our status in the Netherlands if we left the country, "We've already fought so hard and for so long to get approved to stay here. When would we leave the country without a passport or a visa so they could then use it against us in our case?"

I didn't force the issue, and decided to leave it alone until we received our instructions from the U.N. That letter finally did come and it explained exactly what we would have to do for our interview in Frankfurt. It also explained that the trip would be 100% legally documented with the Dutch government and not to worry about leaving the country. It also gave us an exact date when a driver would come to take us for our in-person interview and our medical exams. I called the woman back in Den Haag, and she confirmed that this letter was our permission to leave the Netherlands legally, and that the Dutch government would have records of this interview. It would have no negative bearing on our current case in the Holland. Amin was satisfied with this explanation from the United Nations and felt comfortable leaving the country for this interview after that.

Things seemed to happen so quickly, one right after another after we got that letter. I kept thinking of how strange it was that we were accepted at all. We had gone above and beyond what we had to do for the Netherlands and kept getting denied, yet with the United States we submitted incomplete paperwork and got approval the first time around. As much as I wanted to stay in the Netherlands, I couldn't help but think that maybe God's plan for us included going to the United States. Maybe there was some reason for us to be placed there instead of in Delft, and that's why we had never gotten our approval after seven long years.

Before we knew it the day of our interview arrived and shortly after breakfast time a driver pulled up in front of our home to take us to Frankfurt. It was a cold and snowy day and a trip that should have taken five hours ended up taking nine because of the weather. The driver took us straight to a hotel that had been reserved for us so we could until morning. The next day the drive showed up right on schedule at 9:00am to take us to the United States' embassy. When we got there, we saw a line of people so long that it wrapped around the building. I got a bad feeling in my stomach just thinking of having to wait in that long line.

Luckily the drive told us right away, "Don't worry that's not your line." Then he took us right into a waiting room inside.

We waited almost two hours before they brought us into another room where they provided an interpreter. First they interviewed Amin and after that they interviewed me. At the end of these relatively short interviews the officer said, "Congratulations! From now on you are officially legal residents of the United States!"

I couldn't believe this was all happening so fast. He went on to say, "Very soon after all of your paperwork is completed, and your medical exams are done, you will receive your airline tickets to the United States. We'll send you a notice two weeks prior to your flight so you can prepare."

After hearing these words, I immediately bowed my head and I started to pray giving thanks to God. The officer that had interviewed us said, "Can I ask you what you're doing?"

I told him that I was praying and giving thanks to God for helping us get this approval.

He chuckled and said, "Well you should be giving thanks to me because I'm the one who approved your case."

I smiled and told him, "Yes you are right, but before I came into this room I prayed for God's will to be done, and to place it in your heart to approve us if that was God's will."

He replied, "I envy your faith ma'am, but I still just have one question. How in the world did you become a believer in such a sinful country like Holland? All of the legal drugs and prostitution... how is that possible?"

I laughed and said, "God works in mysterious ways and is beyond our wildest imagination. He uses people and circumstances for His glory in ways we'd never expect."

He took my hands in his and wished us the best of luck for a happy and healthy life in the United States.

We stayed for the rest of the day at the embassy finishing our medical exams, and then at the end of the day the driver took us back to the Netherlands. This time however we did not come back to Holland as refugees without a home, but rather as legal residents of the United States of America. It was surreal after all we had been through to know that we were truly safe from deportation. Finally, after all those years we didn't have to worry that we could be taken in the middle of the night and shipped back to our certain deaths in Iran. It was a tremendous feeling.

We were lost in our heads all the way back to Delft, thinking about what the future might look like. Even in the middle of our relief and extreme happiness knowing that we'd be living in the United States, we still felt torn because we didn't want to leave our dear friends that we had made there. Their level of love and compassion was unlike anything we'd ever known before, and it was crushing in many ways to have to leave that community.

We made the tough decision not to tell our church family and our friends anything about this approval from the U.S. We wanted to wait and make sure our tickets and all the instructions came through before we told them the news. We had been so used to being disappointed that we didn't want to jump the gun and give everyone false hope if the approval was all a mistake by the U.N. We also were afraid of disappointing them by leaving. Everyone had worked so hard. Would they hold it against us for choosing to go to the United States after all their hard work? They had even tried to get us approved for residence in Canada as a backup plan, but we still didn't know how they'd feel about this decision. Finally, we received another denial letter from the Dutch government about a week after our initial interviews in Frankfurt. This is when we made our final, final decision to leave for the United States. Technically we could have appealed this decision once more, but we were so tired of living in uncertainty and felt like God was pushing us this way for a reason.

A few days after our latest denial letter the church had called to tell us that they were going to arrange a meeting with the representative from Canada. This was when I told Amin that it was time for us to tell our friends at the church that we were going to move to the United States. Amin told me that he didn't have the courage to tell them and felt horrible about letting them down and giving up. So, he put that heavy responsibility on my shoulders, and the next Sunday after church we went to Cor's house where the person from Canada was supposed to meet us. When we got there, I decided that this was the best time to go ahead and tell them about everything that had happened, and that we planned on moving to the United States.

I gathered my courage and told them. I explained how it had all started with our incomplete application that we weren't even serious about, but that somehow they had approved us and that we believed that it must be God's will for us to go there. I saw the shock in Cor and Tiny's faces and I was hoping for one of them to start talking so I wouldn't have to talk anymore. The whole time I was trying to hide my eyes from theirs when the guest from Canada chimed in and kindly said, "I am so happy that after these years and these hardships that God has finally found a home for you!"

Tiny also immediately jumped in and had a big smile on her face by then. She said, "It didn't matter to us where you were able to get approved! We only wanted to make sure you had a safe place to live peacefully and happily. If it is God's will that you should move to the United States, then nothing could make us happier!"

Amin was still worried about disappointing them and told them that even though we had our green cards for the United States, that we'd stay in Holland and keep fighting if they wanted us to. He also said that if they wanted us to move to Canada we'd do that too. We were just so thankful for all their love and support that Amin didn't want to let them down or make them feel like we had deceived them in some way.

Cor who had been quiet the whole time finally spoke up with so much love in his voice. He said, "Amin it is a huge blessing to us for you and your family to stay here in the Netherlands, and we have tried for years to get you citizenship here. We have been going through so many obstacles and jumping through so many hoops to get it done, but today I realized something. Today I realized that we can't change the will that God has for you. All the effort that a man can do didn't go anywhere or lead to anything because it is not God's will. If you all move it is going to be very hard for all of us, but seeing you guys struggle with the anxiety of an unsure future is even harder to deal witness. We fought a good fight as a team these past few years, but it's time to accept what God has provided for you."

I looked at Tiny's face and felt so badly. I could see that she was happy for us, but also sad that we'd be leaving. The rest of the day laughed and talked about all our memories that we shared over those past few years. It was heartwarming but bittersweet. I had a strange feeling in my heart when it was time to go home just knowing that we would be separated one day very soon. Separated from these amazing people who had sacrificed so much for us and were always there to support us. I was thinking how I wished that something would have happened so we could have always stayed among this incredible family in Christ. It was a difficult time as much as it was a time of happiness.

While we were waiting for our tickets we had contacted a few other Iranian churches and discovered that there was another Iranian church in the Netherlands located in the city of Rotterdam. We decided to go and visit them before we left for the United States. It was a very small church that met only once a month, and they had a wonderful pastor who was of Assyrian descent. When we were there with them we spoke to the pastor and explained to him that it was in our hearts to start an Iranian church in the city of Delft where we had become believers. We had done some previous research and discovered that there were nearly 1500 Iranians living in Delft, and we wanted so badly to share what she had found with them. We explained to him that we had had bible studies at our house for a while but nothing official, and that we were certain an official Iranian church in Delft would touch and bless a lot of people. We had already spoken to the leaders of our Dutch church in Delft and they had agreed to holding services in Farsi there once a month if we could find someone to give them. We also explained this to the pastor from Rotterdam and asked him if he'd consider coming to Delft once a month to minister to the Iranian people there. This lovely pastor happily accepted this invitation and we all began making plans for these new services.

It was then that we started to send invitations out to all the Iranian families had researched in Delft. The board members of the Dutch church also made it official by announcing it on a Sunday after services. They explained that starting in August we will be having an additional service in Farsi once a month. We were elated to know that the Iranian people living in Delft would have an opportunity to hear the truth about Jesus and learn about God's word.

I was amazed when I realized that it took eight months from the day that we got our green cards for the United States until the day the Iranian church was assembled in our city. When we had our interview in Frankfurt they said we'd be getting our tickets to the United States very fast, but it wasn't. It took an entire eight months. Then once the Iranian church was established we received our tickets that following week. Then we realized that this must have been part of God's plan too. We could stay just long enough to see the first Iranian church service established in Delft before we left.

Finally, the date of our departure had arrived. It was August 24, 1999. That was exactly three weeks after the first Farsi speaking church in our city took place. Today look back on this and truly believe that God wanted to use us for his Glory until the very last second of our stay in the Netherlands.

The weeks before our departure were hectic, and once again our church family came to the rescue. They came in and offered to sell all our belongings and take complete responsibility for it so we wouldn't have to worry about anything left behind. They all came in and bought most of the items themselves. Many of them told us it was so they'd have something to remember us by, and to help put a little extra money in our pockets for the move. They were worried that we'd have to go through even tougher times once we got to the United States so they also decided to throw us a fundraiser before we left. I was so touched by their generosity. It was overwhelming really. They asked me to cook Persian food for the event and it was my honor to do so. It was the least I could do after all they had done for us. I had made Persian food for another fundraiser for orphan children a while back with the church so I thought I'd make the same menu.

As the day approached I realized that this was not only a fundraiser, but that this would be the last meal that all of us would ever share together. After all this time and all the friendships, this was the last time it would ever be like this again. I assumed it would be a smaller party with maybe 50-100 guests, but when I got the final numbers it was between 250-300 people. They told me that there were just so many people that all wanted to be a part of our goodbye party, but they were concerned that it may be too much pressure on me, especially with the new baby. Amin told them not to worry, and promised that he would help and that we'd take care of the entire list. Luckily because I was raised in a big family and there were always people coming in and out of our home for meals, I could handle it if Amin and the kids were there to help me. We started preparing for that night a few days before by going shopping and buying everything that was needed to prepare the feast. I must say that all the heavy work was on the shoulders of Amin and my oldest son. They lifted and hauled everything back to the kitchen, and never complained once. We all made a great team together and it felt so wonderful to give back to this community that had supported us for so long.

The ladies of the church oversaw decorating the tables and the area where'd we be serving food. They had decorated everything so beautifully that anyone that walked in would remark that it looked like a fancy restaurant. We would never forget that nigh. Just to see once again how much love and compassion there was there. It was very special for everyone and we even got to see many of our old friends from Krimpen. In all there were nearly 400 people there! All the guests enjoyed the meal and each one of them gave us a gift to remember them by.

We also found out later that the church had charged an entrance fee for people to come in and had raised the equivalent of over $7,000.00 for us. Agate, Ellen's mother told us that she wanted to come by and purchase all our electronic devices for her home, and Amin told her he wanted to give them to her as a gift. But she ended up paying more for them than we had just to give us money for our move. It was truly incredible to us!

It was so hard for us to leave all of those loving and carrying people behind. This second move to the United States was more difficult for me than the move to the Netherlands had been. We had not only built these incredible bonds with these people but we had also embraced the Dutch way of life. We had worked hard to learn their language and their customs, and the thought of starting over was very difficult and emotional. This second separation was truly much, much harder for all of us.

This family we had in the Netherlands was our spiritual family and we were all part of one body in Jesus Christ. There is nothing stronger than that. Amin would always say that even when he was on the steps of the airplane, if they told him he could become a citizen of the Netherlands, that he would take it instead of leaving.

I remember the last Sunday we were there we went to the Persian Church to say our goodbyes and the pastor was preaching about separation. I knew this message was for Amin and me. The message that God had for us that day was to have faith in God 100% and depend on Him 100%, and if you give something to God to take care of don't try to let Him take care of half of it and you will take care of the other half. Let Him be in control 100% and He will take care of it in His timing.

Don't try to move forward with your thoughts and emotions and go against God's will. Try to accept God's will with humbleness in your life because God loves people who are obedient and will bless them. This was the Message that Amin needed for this second major move. He got down on his knees that day and asked God for forgiveness because ever since we had received our green cards for the U.S.A. he would complain about it instead of being grateful. After hearing this from the pastor that day he surrendered completely to God and said that he would honor whatever God had planned for his life. We had been given such an incredible gift to be able live in the U.S. To so many Persians, America is considered heaven on earth and many of them spent thousands and thousands of dollars trying to get there. I even used to have dreams that I was living in the U.S. ever since I was a young woman. I would have tried to come to the U.S. first if it would have been possible, but it was not. It was only possible through the UN because we had such a hard time in Holland, and we were thankful beyond words for this miracle that God had given us.

Those final days passed by with a lot of sadness and tears, but Amin was tried to keep himself busy with work. He worked until the very last day we were there. On the last night Ida wanted to make the kids their favorite meal and bring dinner to our house so I could finish packing all our stuff. She had made a very delicious tomato soup and brought it over to our home. Her husband Frans and her daughter Lisbeth came with her as well and we had such a nice dinner together. That night after they left I continued cleaning up the apartment. I looked around and realized everything that those walls had witnessed. All our tears and worries, and hopes and dreams. I started to cry thinking of the day that I was so hopeless and I had decided to take the lives of myself and my children. How in that moment the Holy Spirit visited me in that kitchen and brought light into my life and how our lives had changed forever that day?

I also remembered the day that hundreds of Dutch people signed a petition for us to stay in the Netherlands, giving us support even though we were not the same race or from their country. In the end, all the memories we had there made up this incredible plan that God had for our lives. No matter how hard we all tried it was not God's will for our lives. I prayed so hard that night for God to take this sadness out of my heart and to bring us all peace in this horrible time of separation. I could barely sleep that night because of all the anxiety I had over leaving our beloved home.

The day that we stepped foot on the soil of that country we had been outcasts, with no friends or ties to that strange land. We couldn't even speak the language. However, that morning before we left I truly felt like it was home and we were being forced to leave our home. As we walked down the stairs out to the car we realized how many people had come over to see us off. It was incredible. There were a lot of cars in that small parking lot of our apartment complex and they all were waiting in line to say goodbye.

When I fled from my country I found two things that I never expected to find. One was the unconditional love of Christ and the second one was the love of the incredible people we met in our Dutch home. How beautiful it was to find the love of Christ and realize that the love Christ also exists in the hearts of his followers. This was the best gift we received from all our time in Holland, and we took it with us to spread to our new community in our new home in the United States.

Finally, with tear-stained faces we gave every single visitor a hug and thanked them for their love and support. This was not enough for some of them though, and some of them followed us all the way to the airport! In those days, you could see people off right at the gate and that's what many of them did. When it was time to board the plane, it was one of the hardest moments in my entire life. We boarded the plane I sat in my seat and closed my eyes. I could feel all the pain again coursing through my body. It was as if all the pressure from the last seven years had built up to that moment. I was tired and almost right away after we took off I went into a deep sleep. I woke up hours later with the beautiful voice of my daughter Roya crying and when I looked at Amin MJ and Omid they were also deeply sleeping. Soon after the flight attendant announced that we were arriving in Los Angeles. When we got off the plane two people approached us and had noticed us by our bags that had the U.N. symbol on it. They welcomed us to the Unites States and gave us 2 checks for $1300.00 each. One was for that day and the other was dated for a few weeks later. That was how our next adventure began, and even though we had been heartbroken to leave our Dutch family, we were so grateful to finally have a home where we could build our futures without fear.

ABOUT THE AUTHOR

Growing up in Iran, in a traditional Muslim family, Sara never could have imagined that her life would lead her so far outside the confines of the only home she'd ever known. She watched as the world around her changed after the Islamic Revolution took hold, and after years of tribulation she and her family would risk everything to make a new start in The Netherlands.

This book is the true account of their journey out of Iran and subsequent years in Europe where they would live as refugees. Through one struggle after another, they stayed strong as a family and found an unwavering level of love and support from the Dutch friends they met in their new home. It was through these precious friendships that God's plan for their lives would be revealed. They would go on to become the first Muslim family ever to be baptized in a historic Christian Church and dedicate their lives to Christ.

This inspirational story not only illustrates the power of prayer and the impact of kindness, but also reminds us that we are all God's children and that it is HE that connects us. From all corners of the globe, from all walks of life the Gospel can break down barriers and heal old wounds to bring His children together.

If you would like to contact the author please email

Lostrefugeesfoundinchrist@gmail.com

eilijk, maar we moeten sterk zijn"

uwen in asielzoeke trum De Stuw

rouwen de. Ze neen en op hun oor een ijk, de gt zijn is uit- eral de kie' is soepel

el sterk esprekje n aantal e tijd in n Hotel

middag anks de Bedrij- hotelka- bij vier zetten. met een heegla- tussen ar 'keu- e naast

zij de dt geg- van de te heb- oek om het ge- ar wei-

nist zu Op het kinde- op wat recre- jonge k wat

In de kleine hotelkamer wordt met de asielvrouwen gepraat.

één vraag en die is: hoe is het om als vrouw in een asielzoekerscentrum te moeten verblijven.

„Heel moeilijk, maar je moet sterk zijn'', is aanvankelijk het resolute antwoord. Een antwoord waarachter heel veel leed, ingehouden boosheid en heimwee schuilgaat, zo wordt in het volgende uur duidelijk.

Want zoals overal ter wereld zijn ook deze vrouwen hun mannen blindelings gevolgd, ook toen besloten werd om de geboortegrond om wat voor reden te verlaten. Heimwee is er naar wat ze achterlieten. Er wordt om hulp gevraagd bij het leggen van contacten met achtergebleven familieleden.

De krabbel van de fotograaf maakt iets goed.

ven en een eigen woonruimte krijgen toegewezen, waardoor het gezin weer op zichzelf is. Het wachten is op een kans op een betere toekomst. Die kans denken

ke bevolking.

Regelmatig

Contacten die voor de één wat

The Refugee Center

C and B Blenk

Cor and Tiny – Dr. de Reuver and Julie

Pim and Fiet Fisher

Franz and Ida

New Church in Delft

Made in the USA
San Bernardino, CA
13 September 2017